I am so delighted with R. T. Kendall's book *The Presence of God*. Its importance is unmistakable because we need to experience and recognize God's presence. I like the in-depth scripture RT gives you to see, feel, and to know, but I also like how he reveals the sovereignty of God. We long for God's presence. We long to know Him in a more intimate way. *The Presence of God* will lead you into that sweet intimacy. R. T. Kendall is my favorite author. I love his books, and this one is my new favorite.

—MARILYN HICKEY
PRESIDENT, MARILYN HICKEY MINISTRIES

Many books about knowing God are actually doctrinal studies that ought to be entitled *Knowing About God*. RT's latest work really is about knowing and experiencing God. As a wise, balanced, and practical book, it will be a valuable resource for all who hunger for the presence of God in the churches.

—DR. MICHAEL EATON
PASTOR-AT-LARGE, CHRISCO FELLOWSHIP

This book will cause you to think deeper on the Word and create a stir within your heart to hunger for more of God. The teaching of the conscious and unconscious presence of God is a faith builder regardless of our denominational background.

—DANIEL HO
SENIOR PASTOR, INTERNATIONAL CHURCH OF SHANGHAI

I found deep encouragement and comfort in this book. In Jesus Christ, God is with us—when we feel Him and when we don't. Yet we can hunger and thirst for Him, and often

experience by the Spirit those precious foretastes of what it will be like to be with Him forever.

—Craig S. Keener
F. M. and Ada Thompson Professor of Biblical Studies, Asbury Theological Seminary

Perhaps the best measure of the anointing on a book is its ability to draw both positive reviews and negative fire from multiple directions. By that calibration *The Presence of God* by R. T. Kendall is absolutely not to be missed. Argue with it if you must. Praise it if you will, but by all means read this book.

—Mark Rutland
Former President of Oral Roberts University

R. T. Kendall is a superb communicator—one of the most remarkable preachers and writers of our time. After a lifetime of ministry, his words are always full of wisdom, power, and relevance.

—Nicky Gumbel
Vicar, Holy Trinity Brompton

Bro. RT, as we affectionately call him, is a friend and mentor. While we do not have the liberty to meet as regularly as we want to, each time we do, there is such a bond that I can only describe as a kingdom connection. *The Presence of God* is a must-have. I got hooked the moment I started on it. Bro. RT has such a flair and anointing for writing that he makes reading an absolute delight. This is a definite home run.

—Yang Tuck Yoong
Senior Pastor,
Cornerstone Community Church, Singapore
Director, Bible College of Wales, Swansea

Among his plethora of books, this may be R. T. Kendall's very best. This is no small thought in light of his more-then-sixty tomes. We can always depend on RT to bring to the table an ordered presentation with new, heretofore unheralded thoughts. Simply profound and profoundly simple! It occurred to me that this whole presentation is, in one word, *kingdom*! I may be the loudest voice in RT's huge fan club! Thanks again, my dear friend!

—JACK TAYLOR
DIMENSIONS MINISTRIES

I've really enjoyed reading RT's book *The Presence of God*. It has caused me to stop, look, and listen for the Lord and to be more aware of His presence in my life. I think you'll be blessed as I have been.

—RICKY SKAGGS
COUNTRY SINGER RECORDING ARTIST

Nothing is more important, more desired, more missed than the presence of God. This book is grounded in Scripture yet immensely practical. It is a masterful job from a gifted teacher helping each of us Jesus followers live a life in and with God's presence.

—DAVID MCQUEEN
PASTOR, BELTWAY CHURCH

Dr. R. T. Kendall has written a very balanced book on a subject that needs to be explored more thoroughly by the body of Christ. He is uniquely qualified to write a book on such an important topic combining thoughtful biblical scholarship with experiential knowledge. You will find his insights enlightening and challenging at the same time.

This is a must-read for all who long for the manifest presence of God!

—SAMUEL SONG
SENIOR PASTOR, SOLOMON'S PORCH

Diving into an R. T. Kendall book is a spiritual delight. And now RT has brought dessert, a truly honest and real treatment of that greatest of all rewards—God's presence. The reader can relax in this book, confident in RT's fervent and unwavering grasp of sound doctrine that results in all the more appreciation of the unlimited ways in which our God can relate to us in love and power. *The Presence of God* is a safe and exhilarating guide to a whole world of experience that is our inheritance.

—ROLLAND AND HEIDI BAKER
IRIS GLOBAL, MOZAMBIQUE, AFRICA

The Presence of God exposes RT's contagious passion for the glory of God. Reading it will help you appreciate God's presence with you at all times and make you hungry for more of him.

—COLIN DYE
SENIOR MINISTER, KENSINGTON TEMPLE

THE
PRESENCE
GOD
OF

THE
PRESENCE
GOD
OF

R.T. KENDALL

CHARISMA
HOUSE

Most CHARISMA HOUSE BOOK GROUP products are available at special quantity discounts for bulk purchase for sales promotions, premiums, fund-raising, and educational needs. For details, write Charisma House Book Group, 600 Rinehart Road, Lake Mary, Florida 32746, or telephone (407) 333-0600.

THE PRESENCE OF GOD by R. T. Kendall
Published by Charisma House
Charisma Media/Charisma House Book Group
600 Rinehart Road
Lake Mary, Florida 32746
www.charismahouse.com

Unless otherwise noted, all Scripture quotations are taken from the Modern English Version. Copyright © 2014 by Military Bible Association. Used by permission. All rights reserved.

Scripture quotations marked ESV are from the Holy Bible, English Standard Version. Copyright © 2001 by Crossway Bibles, a division of Good News Publishers. Used by permission.

Scripture quotations marked KJV are from the King James Version of the Bible.

Scripture quotations marked NIV are taken from the Holy Bible, New International Version®, NIV®. Copyright © 1973, 1978, 1984, 2011 by Biblica, Inc.™ Used by permission of Zondervan. All rights reserved worldwide. www.zondervan.com. The "NIV" and "New International Version" are trademarks registered in the United States Patent and Trademark Office by Biblica, Inc.™

Scripture quotations marked NLT are from the Holy Bible, New Living Translation, copyright © 1996, 2004, 2007. Used by permission of Tyndale House Publishers, Inc., Wheaton, IL 60189. All rights reserved.

Cover design by Vincent Pirozzi
Design Director: Justin Evans

Visit the author's website at www.rtkendallministries.com.

Library of Congress Cataloging-in-Publication Data:
An application to register this book for cataloging has been submitted to the Library of Congress.
International Standard Book Number: 978-1-62999-157-3
E-book ISBN: 978-1-62999-158-0

While the author has made every effort to provide accurate Internet addresses at the time of publication, neither the publisher nor the author assumes any responsibility for errors or for changes that occur after publication.

17 18 19 20 21 — 9 8 7 6 5 4 3 2 1
Printed in the United States of America

To
Grant and Jenni

In your presence there is fullness of joy.
—Psalm 16:11, esv

Contents

Special Recommendation

Dr. R. T. Kendall is a highly respected Bible teacher, pastor, thinker, and writer not only in the United States but also very especially so in the United Kingdom. For years he was the pastor of Westminster Chapel, only a few yards from Buckingham Palace. He was a blessing to all of England. The pulpit had been occupied by great preachers of the past, such as Dr. G. Campbell Morgan and Dr. D. Martyn Lloyd-Jones, and he magnificently followed in their footsteps.

RT has taken a strong stand on the authority of Holy Scripture and has taught it with joy, with enthusiasm, with great biblical integrity, and with historic insights.

I thank God for every occasion in which we can be blessed, taught, and enriched spiritually by the teaching of the Word of God by our friend, brother, and fellow servant, Dr. R. T. Kendall. I pray that this book will enrich your spiritual life too.

—Luis Palau
International Evangelist

Foreword

EVERY AUGUST DR. R. T. and Louise Kendall bring messages of hope to our northern New Jersey church. My husband, David, and I always look forward to their arrival and the spiritual nurturing they provide to our congregation. The Kendalls' summer stopovers are fast becoming a joy-filled tradition at Christ Church. One thing we most anticipate is getting a copy of RT's latest book, especially when it is about the Holy Spirit's work in the life of today's Christ followers. This is something our church values. Consequently, when RT asked me to write the foreword for *The Presence of God*, I was delighted, humbled, and honored.

There are some books you read and as a result gain critical knowledge. Then there are other books that read you. *The Presence of God* undoubtedly falls into both of these categories, but especially the latter. I believe that you will find this to be true. As each chapter, paragraph, and sentence unfolds, it will scrape the underbelly of your soul, exposing things that are unhealthy theologically and culturally. Things such as flawed perspectives and blemishes you didn't even know were there, or hidden, slippery things such as secular perceptions of spirituality and creepy, malformed notions of our intimacy with the Holy Spirit.

With these very serious forces at work within us, our underbellies need some light. Reading this book will provide that light! You'll find that reading this book is well worth your time, for freedom, clarity, light, and deliverance are on every page. In *The Presence of God* truth and the wisdom of the Scriptures and RT's God-soaked life act as holy scalpels, cutting back our deadness to the Spirit (Heb. 4:12). The blade of his pastoral wisdom slices away, unveiling fresh eyes for the pursuit of a healthier relationship with the Comforter, Teacher, and Guide. So discerning are its principles that after each chapter, I found myself looking inward, as well as upward. I needed to know, "Marlinda, how are you and the Spirit getting along? Are you near to Him, even though He is always near to you? Are you friends, companions, or distant relatives?" Lastly, I asked, "Dear God, am I alive in Your presence or alive in our culture's false path to spiritual power?"

These are convicting questions for sure. Thankfully, threads of mercy and hope are generously sewn throughout *The Presence of God* and will repeatedly resuscitate—even resurrect you—from inward areas of deadness to God's nearness. For He *is* near. And this powerful treatise comes to give us greater Spirit consciousness. Read it. Imbibe it daily, prayerfully, and humbly.

—MARLINDA IRELAND, DMIN
CHRIST CHURCH
COFOUNDER AND ASSISTANT PASTOR

Preface

SEVERAL YEARS AGO Pastor Grant Brewster purchased my book *In Pursuit of His Glory*—an autobiographical account of my twenty-five years at Westminster Chapel. He had not heard of me or the chapel. He merely liked the title; it captured his heart because he too was in pursuit of God's glory! After he read the book, he got in touch with me and invited me to preach at his church.

Although he liked my book, he really thought it would be about the presence of God. He has kindly invited me to his church, The Island Church, many times. He and his wife, Jenni, have become good friends. But he keeps pleading with me to write a book specifically on the presence of God.

Here it is, Grant.

Introduction

I HEARD A RING at the door of the Castle Lane entrance to Westminster Chapel and found Billy Graham on the doorstep. For the next hour and forty-five minutes we had an uninterrupted conversation in my vestry. I had to pinch myself that I was actually in the presence of one of the most famous and admired men in the world. When I got home, my wife, Louise, asked me, "What was it like to spend time with Billy Graham?" I paused and thought and tears came to my eyes as I said, "He is so uncomplicated, so simple."

Have you ever been in the presence of greatness? Whether it was a famous person or one quite unknown, did you feel you were with someone whose presence was impactful and unforgettable? What did this person's presence actually do for you?

Or I might ask, What would the presence of Billy Graham do for me if I could never tell it to anybody? The truth is, I was in fact edified by his visit. He shared things with me that I have applied in my life again and again since that time over thirty years ago. That said, I used to ask the members of Westminster Chapel, "How many of you would want to have tea with Her Majesty the Queen if you could never tell it to anyone?" Being in the presence of famous people is usually of no consequence except for the fun of telling it—and impressing your friends.

But being in the presence of God is fulfilling in itself, even if you never told it to a single person.

A good friend and pastor told me of an extraordinary incident in his life that lasted "less than ten seconds." He was in a hotel in Brazil. "As I walked from one room to the other, there was a sudden sense of the presence of God." The joy was incalculable. He said, "For that very brief moment, I would have endured *anything*." He referred to various trials he has had over the years, including him and his wife raising their daughter who remained in diapers and never walked or talked and died at age sixteen. "Anything," he stressed. It made me ask, whatever will heaven be like? It reminds me of the line from E. E. Hewitt's hymn "When We All Get to Heaven": "Just one glimpse of Him in glory will the toils of life repay." One glimpse will do it then. One glimpse will do it now.

I should make it clear that this book is not primarily about seeing God, although one must not rule out that possibility: God has surprising ways of showing up! However, this book is rather about the *sense*—the consciousness and awareness—of God's presence. My friend did not see anything in that hotel room; he *felt* God's presence for a few seconds.

So one wonders, whatever will it be like when we get to heaven? I reckon that our present sufferings are not worth comparing with the glory that will be revealed in us (Rom. 8:18).

This book will conclude with the presence of God in heaven, and yet we may experience the presence of God now *because* we are seated with Christ "in the heavenly places" (Eph. 2:6). Therefore what follows is about the presence of God on earth—in the here and now. I am writing about the same God who dwells in heaven, who *chooses* to manifest Himself to lowly creatures on earth. For the glory of the Lord fills the universe.

To what extent may you and I feel God's presence today? is the question. And the answer is, far more than many of us have realized. First Corinthian 2:9 says, "Eye has not seen, nor ear heard, nor has it entered into the heart of man the things which God has prepared for those who love Him," and it is usually quoted with reference to what it will be like when we get to heaven. And yet the following verse says, "But God has revealed them to us by His Spirit" (v. 10). The Holy Spirit *can bring heaven forward.* Some Puritans called this experience heaven on earth. In the words of another great hymn, "Jesus, the Very Thought of Thee," by Bernard of Clairvaux, "The love of Jesus, what it is, none but His loved ones know."

What is the difference between feeling God's presence now and being in His presence in heaven? The answer is that when we get to heaven, we will be glorified. "We will all be changed." We will be "imperishable," our transformed bodies immortal (1 Cor. 15:51–53, NIV). One glimpse of Jesus's face will make us like Him (1 John 3:2). Glorification will mean the absence of sin, temptation, sorrow, tears, death, pain, insecurity, and worry. The "former things" will have "passed away" (Rev. 21:4). Seeing the face of Jesus directly and immediately will make this happen. Feeling His presence now is but a taste of the glory to come.

This book therefore is about the presence of God before we get to heaven, while we are in our mortal, perishable, "lowly bodies" and when we are still sinful, insecure, vulnerable, and carnal (Phil. 3:21, NIV). Can people like that truly experience God Himself before we get to heaven? Yes.

The purpose of this book is not only to explain how experiencing the presence of God is possible; I also hope to show how you may see this for yourself in your mind and feel this in your heart. I want to show that you may experience the presence of God in a manner by which you know you have not been deceived or imagining things.

These things said, my book would not be complete if I did not include strange manifestations of God's presence. I have often heard it said that the Holy Spirit is a gentleman. That sounds good and puts some people at ease, but I am not sure that the Holy Spirit is always a "gentleman." I am not sure that God is "seeker friendly." Like it or not, God sometimes offends the sophisticated by the manner in which He may choose to show up. He offends the mind to reveal our hearts. He may manifest Himself in a way that will be totally acceptable to many traditional Christians. He may also choose to test our faith by the untraditional way in which He may reveal Himself.

But remember this: no experience of God—whether miracle, healing, sign, or wonder—will utterly remove the need for faith in this present life. Do not think that God will raise anybody's sense of His presence to the height that he or she no longer needs faith. Faith is the assurance of things hoped for and the evidence of things not seen (Heb. 11:1). What makes faith *faith* is believing without seeing. And yet even some of the eleven disciples who *saw* the risen Jesus still doubted. "When they saw him, they worshipped him. But some doubted" (Matt. 28:17).

And yet I will admit that sometimes God may make Himself so real that—for a while—you feel you don't need faith. But that feeling will not last indefinitely. The memory of it, however, will last and will keep you encouraged. For example, as I will show in this book, I myself experienced the living Christ interceding for me at the right hand of God for a few moments many years ago. I can remember it being as real to me as anything I ever saw in my life, and the memory of it is very encouraging to me.

I pray that this book will be a means of motivating you to a closer walk with God and that this closer walk with God will result in *you* experiencing His glorious presence.

CHAPTER 1

The Unconscious Presence of God

Surely the LORD is in this place,
and I did not know it.
—GENESIS 28:16

Did not our hearts burn within us while
He talked to us on the way and while
He opened the Scriptures to us?
—LUKE 24:32

To FEEL THE presence of God is wonderful. I will not even come close to describing what it feels like in this book, for His presence is greater than anything that can be said about it. Any attempt to describe God's presence will at best be like looking at pictures of a place you've never been. When I looked at photographs of London's Big Ben, Niagara Falls, the Grand Canyon, the Sea of Galilee, the Mount of Olives, the Golden Gate Bridge, the Empire State Building, Hong Kong Harbor, the Swiss Alps, the Kremlin, the Eiffel Tower, and inside Yankee Stadium, I never truly understood what being there would be like.

Perception is one thing, but seeing the real thing is quite another.

The same is true when you hear of famous people or

seeing their photographs and then meet them in person. In my case, it was like meeting my baseball hero Joe DiMaggio or great theologians and ministers such as Martyn Lloyd-Jones, J. I. Packer, or John Stott. I have even been privileged to meet a few other well-known people outside the church. I can remember meeting each of these individuals for the first time. My perception in advance of meeting these people was one thing, but seeing them face-to-face was quite another.

People sometimes ask me, "Have you ever met the queen?" Answer: no. But I was invited to be very near her—three or four feet away—when I was at Oxford. You don't speak to Her Majesty unless she speaks to you. She didn't speak to me, so I just looked. I was not prepared for how extraordinarily beautiful she is. No photograph does her justice.

What would you expect to feel—or think—if you experienced directly the presence of God? Do you think you would immediately recognize His presence? What if God showed up in more than one way? And what if He showed up in a manner for which there is no known precedent? What if God agreed to manifest Himself to you on the condition you could never tell?

Most of this book will be about the conscious presence of God and the surprising ways He may choose to turn up.

Prayer Covenant

When I was at Westminster Chapel, I introduced a prayer covenant. Over three hundred people signed up to pray daily for certain requests, including this petition: "We pray for the manifestation of the glory of God in our midst along with an ever-increasing openness in us to the manner in which He chooses to show up." Why did I word it like that? It is because God may show up in more than one way. I knew something about many reports of the Cane Ridge Revival in Bourbon County, Kentucky, in 1801. My greatest fear was that God might repeat that sort of thing to the dignified and stiff-upper-lip Brits in Westminster Chapel. People fell to the ground by the hundreds at Cane Ridge and remained that way for hours. I therefore felt it necessary to prepare the way for the most extreme sort of manifestations that might come to us. For some His presence may seem strange, bizarre, and embarrassing. Or perhaps God would spare us controversy and grant us a sense of His presence that would be self-authenticating, similar to seeing the Grand Canyon for the first time.

What I feared—or wanted—never came to pass.

And yet we *did* see the manifestation of God's glory. God gets as much glory when He does not appear to show up as He does when He manifests Himself overtly. His unconscious presence is as real and orchestrated as when we feel Him.

The two men on the road to Emmaus thought they were speaking to a total stranger when the resurrected Jesus showed up to them. It was after they recognized Him and He disappeared that they realized, upon reflection, how they did indeed feel His presence: "Did not our hearts burn within us while He talked to us on the way?" (Luke 24:32).

Sometimes I look back on our twenty-five years at

Westminster Chapel and conclude that I failed. And yet I can also look back on certain moments when there was an undoubted manifestation of God's presence. There is nothing unspectacular about people being converted or healed or feeling great joy.

What I hoped for—or even feared—kept me from seeing what God was indeed doing before our eyes.

The truth is that God may be at work during the times of His unconscious presence the same as when He clearly shows up!

One may see the Lord and feel nothing at the moment—just as the two men on the road to Emmaus. And yet John wrote, "When I saw Him, I fell at His feet as though I were dead" (Rev. 1:17).

God has a way of showing up in multitudinous, unpredictable, and unprecedented ways. But we must learn to appreciate His unconscious presence if we are truly to enjoy His conscious presence.

I would do you no favor if I wrote only about the conscious presence of God in this book. Indeed, one of my goals is to make you as appreciative of the unconscious presence of God as His conscious presence. This is the way faith is built. When Peter, James, and John saw Jesus transfigured on the mountain—and they saw His glory alongside the appearances of Moses and Elijah—Peter immediately said, "Lord, it is good for us to be here" (Matt. 17:4). Quite. Oh yes. When God reveals Himself like that, we want such a moment to go on and on and on. But they had to come down from the mountain (v. 9). They had so much more to learn.

One glimpse of the glory of the Lord here below will

almost always be followed by struggle, teaching, pain, learning, suffering, and the pursuit of the knowledge of God. "My people are destroyed for lack of knowledge," said an ancient prophet (Hos. 4:6). "We must go through many hardships to enter the kingdom of God" (Acts 14:22, NIV). I will never forget the comment of a ninety-year-old woman—one of my mother's mentors back in Springfield, Illinois—who said: "I have served the Lord so long that I can hardly tell the difference between a blessing and a trial."

This is why James could say, "Count it all joy" when we face all kinds of trials (James 1:2). Paul said: "We rejoice in hope of the glory of God" (Rom. 5:2). Yes. "But we *also* boast in tribulation, knowing that tribulation produces patience, patience produces character, and character produces hope. And hope does not disappoint, because the love of God is shed abroad in our hearts by the Holy Spirit who has been given to us" (vv. 3–5, emphasis added).

Taking the bad with the good is what builds faith. And what we at first thought was bad turns out to be *good* when we become willing to come down from the mountain to see the next thing God wants us to learn. "All things work together for *good* to them who love God, to those who are the called according to His purpose" (Rom. 8:28, emphasis added).

Jacob

At first Jacob felt nothing. He had just left home and was running from his brother, Esau, who was bent on killing him. He grew up knowing he was the grandson of the great Abraham, but he was no match for Abraham. He could never live up to the status of a legend like that. Not only that, but also Jacob knew he had done everything wrong: he had tricked his brother, Esau, into selling his birthright, and he deceived his father, Isaac, to get the patriarchal blessing. He was now running for his life.

Where was God in all this? Jacob reached "a certain place" (Gen. 28:11). As we will see below, Jacob prayed. He felt nothing when he arrived there. There was nothing spectacular about this place. There were no signs that said, "You will treasure this place one day." He was tired and scared. He needed to sleep. Expecting absolutely nothing, he took a stone for a pillow, put it under his head, and lay down to sleep. And then God stepped in—with a dream. It was a dream that revealed that the God of Abraham was now Jacob's God. The words given to Jacob were almost too good to be true. Jacob would never be the same again (vv. 11–15).

A "certain place" was where Jacob felt nothing at first; he had no sense of God, no hope, and no purpose in life. But that place became pivotal not only for Jacob but also for countless millions over the succeeding centuries. It is called Bethel, which means "the house of God."

Bethel became a symbol of both the unconscious presence of God and the conscious presence of God. "Surely the LORD is in this place, and I did not know it," he said (Gen. 28:16). This means that the house of God is huge, so big that it has room for all of God that there is—room for both the conscious presence of God and His unconscious presence.

The unconscious presence of God only means that we

feel nothing when He is present. His presence is very real—very real indeed. But a sense of Him is *kept* from us. We feel nothing whatsoever, but He is there as much as when we feel Him.

We must learn to respect God when He does not appear to reveal Himself. We must honor Him when we feel nothing. We must worship Him when we are tired and afraid. In our weakest moment—yes, even in our most embarrassing moment when we feel we have done everything wrong and nothing right—God is absolutely *there.* "I will never leave you, nor forsake you" (Heb. 13:5), He promises. Or as Jesus put it, "I am with you always, even to the end of the age" (Matt. 28:20).

Can you accept this? Do you believe this? It means that God is with us whether or not we feel Him—twenty-four hours a day, three hundred sixty-five days a year.

We need to remember this in *all* aspects of our lives. It can be in a time of prayer or a time of frivolity. It is true when we are struggling to hear from God or when we are having fun. It is true when we have messed up and our closest friends or loved ones misunderstand us or reject us.

Back in 1956 I made decisions that would change my life totally. Those decisions meant a different perspective, a different theology, a different denomination, and a different set of friends. My family—my dad, my grandmother, my aunts and uncles—were distraught; they were convinced I had gone completely off the rails and was headed for certain disaster. Only one of my relatives stood up for me—Grandpa McCurley (for some reason he was always my favorite relative)—saying, "I'm for him, right or wrong." That was what I needed. I needed someone who would stand up for me.

God is like that. He is for us—right or wrong.

Therefore, we must not panic when we don't feel God's presence. We must not give up when we feel nothing. For when we feel nothing, God is at work. When we don't feel His presence, He is there—the unconscious presence of God. Learn to recognize this, and honor such a moment, no matter how long it lasts.

The unconscious presence of God may be the best explanation for any number of occurrences: when you are praying and reading your Bible alone; when you are doing all you know to do to please Him; when you are busy and conscientious in the work of the Lord—in any kind of ministry, for example, law, nursing, medicine, parenting, accounting. In my case, preaching.

This experience has happened to me more than once. In one particular instant, instead of enjoying great liberty and a sense of the anointing of the Holy Spirit in preaching, I struggled. My mouth was dry, and I could feel beads of perspiration on my head. But I continued, sticking it out. I was relieved when the sermon was finally over. I then walked down the steps of the historic pulpit at Westminster Chapel, hurrying to the vestry to be alone. I said to myself, "If this is the best I can do, I should get out of the ministry," feeling deserted by the same God who, I thought, called me to be the minister there.

But God in His infinite mercy stepped in moments later. After the service there was a knock on the door of the vestry. One of our deacons said someone wanted to see me. A man walked into the vestry. Lo and behold, he had just been converted through my pitiful sermon moments before! He had no idea how I felt about my preaching that day; he also had little idea how joyous I felt that God overruled my lack of faith and saved this man.

More than twenty years ago I preached in a large auditorium in Bournemouth, England. The event was put on by a group called Easter People, and I felt honored to be there. I preached to perhaps two thousand people what I thought would be an appropriate sermon. But when I finished, no one said a word. Every preacher I know in this world *loves* a cheerful word after he has preached his heart out. At least "Thank you for your word" (which may camouflage the person's true feelings), "That was good," or something similar. But on that night? Nothing. Embarrassed, I hung around for ten minutes even though I had a two-hour drive back to London. I wanted just *one* encouraging word that I had not messed up. Nothing came, and I left for London.

A few weeks ago—just before beginning this very book—a woman came up to me to say she heard me preach at an Easter People event in Bournemouth and had been converted on that very night. I was not prepared for that pleasant word. She had no idea how distraught I was that night—twenty years prior.

The Lord was there, but I felt nothing.

Have you ever felt deserted by God? The biblical expression for this feeling is the *hiding of God's face.* "Truly You are a God who hides Yourself, O God of Israel, the Savior" (Isa. 45:15), a common occurrence that we will look at in chapter 2.

Two Ways of Understanding the Presence of God

As I have already said, God's presence may be understood in two ways: His unconscious presence and His conscious presence. Many of us tend not to appreciate God's unconscious presence; rather, we long for His conscious presence—when He clearly shows up.

The theological term that is relevant to both ways we experience God's presence is the *omnipresence* of God. God is everywhere; there is no place where He isn't:

> Where shall I go from Your spirit, or where shall I flee from Your presence? If I ascend to heaven, You are there; if I make my bed in Sheol, You are there. If I take the wings of the morning and dwell at the end of the sea, even there Your hand shall guide me, and Your right hand shall take hold of me. If I say, "Surely the darkness shall cover me, and the light shall be as night about me," even the darkness is not dark to You, but the night shines as the day, for the darkness is like light to You.
>
> —PSALM 139:7–12

Theologians speak of the "three big *O*s": God's *omnipotence* (that He is all-powerful), His *omniscience* (that He knows everything) and His *omnipresence* (that He is everywhere). His omnipresence not only means that God is everywhere—His glory fills the universe and all He has made—but it also means that we cannot run from God. Jonah found this to be true. God told him, "Go to Nineveh." Jonah said, "No." He rose to flee "from the presence of the LORD" (Jon. 1:2–3) but found such a notion impossible to fulfill. Wherever Jonah went, there was God!

Are you trying to run from God? Give up! It is a hopeless venture.

That fact that you may not *feel* God does not mean He is not there. The fact that you don't even *believe* in God will not cause Him to go away. If we believe not, said Paul, God "remains faithful; He cannot deny Himself" (2 Tim. 2:13). Let's look at some Scripture pertaining to God's omnipresence:

> Can a man hide himself in secret places so that I do not see him? says the LORD. Do I not fill heaven and earth? says the LORD.
> —JEREMIAH 23:24

> The eyes of the LORD are in every place, keeping watch on the evil and the good.
> —PROVERBS 15:3

> But will God indeed dwell on the earth? See, heaven and the heaven of heavens cannot contain You.
> —1 KINGS 8:27

Never underestimate how near God is to you when you feel nothing. When I first met missionary Jackie Pullinger in Hong Kong, she described how she decided to pray in the Spirit for fifteen minutes every day "by the clock." She added: "I felt nothing. But those were the days when I began to see conversions in the Walled City. When I saw the Lord changing people then I was full of feeling."

Jacob was no match for his grandfather Abraham. He could not have known that one day the phrase "the God of Abraham, Isaac, and Jacob" would become a cliché in Israel—and that Jacob's new name, *Israel*, would become the name of a great nation. It all began at Bethel, where Jacob at first felt nothing, only to realize that God was there and he did not know it.

Jacob became a symbol of the sovereign grace of God in more ways than one. He was an example of a scoundrel who was loved by God. "I have loved Jacob" (Mal. 1:2; see Rom. 9:13). There was absolutely nothing in Jacob that deserved to be loved by God. He had done everything wrong. He knew it and was running scared. The last thing he expected was for God to show up and then reveal wonderful plans for Jacob.

Are you running scared? Are you afraid for God to show up? Do you fear that if God were to show up He would certainly judge you?

Bethel Yesterday, Ramallah Today

One day when I visited Yasser Arafat in Ramallah, it hit me as I entered the city that I was in ancient Bethel! Yes, Ramallah today and Bethel of biblical times are very near the same geographical location. I said to Arafat, thinking I might be telling him something he did not know: "Do you realize this is Bethel?" He did in fact know this and was very pleased about it.

There I was—literally—at Bethel, the very place where God manifested his glory to Jacob; indeed, where Jacob at first felt nothing insofar as the presence of God was concerned. I tried to take it in. "Yes," I said to myself, "I am exactly where God first met with Jacob." It was also the exact place Jacob had been commanded to return to when his heart had become cold and detached from God's purpose. Jacob obeyed and announced to his family, "Put away the foreign gods that are among you. Purify yourselves and change your clothes. Let us arise and go up to Bethel, and there I will make an altar to God, who *answered me* in the day of my distress and has *been with me* wherever I have gone" (Gen. 35:1–3, emphasis added). Note the two phrases I have italicized in Jacob's words. The first is "who *answered me* in the day of my distress." That is how we know Jacob was actually praying when he came to the previously mentioned "certain place." The second phrase, "[who] has *been with me* wherever I have gone," is Jacob acknowledging God's presence with him. This includes the times when Jacob was mistreated by Laban (Gen. 31), when he demonstrated how he still feared that Esau was bent on killing him (Gen. 32–33), and when his daughter Dinah had drifted into the world and lost her purity (Gen. 34). His family was disunited, and Jacob seemed to have lost control of them (Gen. 34:30–31). But when God told him, "Go up to Bethel," those words were music to his ears (Gen. 35:1). His family obeyed, and as they set out, "the terror of God was on the cities that were around them, and they did not pursue the sons of Jacob" (v. 5).

This tells me that if the church today would go back to Bethel, a sense of the fear of God would fall on the world, which at the moment does not respect the church as it might.

God demonstrated to unworthy Jacob the truth of His sheer mercy and grace. The faithfulness of God seems too good to be true. I sometimes say, "Unless the gospel you heard preached seemed 'too good to be true,' you haven't heard it yet! But when you say to yourself, 'That's too good to be true,' that is when you heard it." This means we are saved apart from works and kept apart from works (Eph. 2:8–9). Yes, we are loved with an everlasting love (Jer. 31:3).

A man came to see me in the vestry at Westminster Chapel one evening. He was an admitted backslider. He told me he had been saved many years before, but he knew he was no longer a Christian because of the depth of the sin in his life. I said to him, "What hope do you have of going to heaven?"

He replied, "No hope at all."

I asked him, "If you were to stand before God—and you will—and He were to ask you, 'Why should I let you into my heaven?' what would you say?"

He answered, "I have no hope whatever—only that Jesus died for me on the cross."

I looked at him and asked again, "Are you saying that your only hope of heaven is the blood that Jesus shed for you two thousand years ago when He died on the cross?"

"Oh, yes," he said again." But I have wandered so far from God."

I said to him, "What if I were to tell you that you are as saved as I am?"

He looked at me and said, "Could that possibly be true?" I said to him, "It is true. You are as saved as I am, for the only hope that I have is the shed blood of Jesus Christ."

I never saw anything like it. He came alive. His face lit up. It was the greatest news he could possibly hear.

"I can't believe that God loves me that much." He added,

"This makes me want to serve Him, live for Him. I am so sorry for my sins. I want to give my life back to Him." He then said, as if double-checking on what he thought he heard, "You are saying to me that I have been a saved person all these years?"

"That's exactly what I am saying."

The man walked out as happy—I would have thought—as the day he was first converted.

I will not be surprised if some readers will disagree with what I said to him. I do understand. I myself was brought up to believe that if I sinned in any way, I lost my salvation and was then on the road to hell. I had an epiphany one day through the sweetest and most glorious manifestation of the presence of Christ I have ever experienced. With it came an infallible assurance that I was eternally saved. I have never looked back.

Here's the important point I want to make regarding this man who came into my vestry. I knew I could easily lead him back to the Lord. That was why he came in. He was clearly being dealt with. He was *so* sorry for his failure. I could have given him the sinner's prayer and he would have prayed it eagerly, no doubt about it. But then he would have based his assurance on his good works instead of the mercy of God.

The thought that the unconscious presence of God had been with him all those years blew his mind away. I quoted the psalm to him, "If I make my bed in hell, behold, thou art there" (Ps. 139:8, KJV). The overwhelming sense of God's mercy made him want to straighten his life out far more—in my view—than if I treated him as a person who needed to be saved.

Does this mean that all people who pray the sinner's prayer or make a profession of faith are eternally saved? No. This is because such a prayer can be prayed in a cerebral manner and not from the heart. The promise of salvation is to those who believe in their *hearts* (Rom. 10:9–10).

When Billy Graham preached at Westminster Chapel in May 1984, some eighty people went forward, including a famous businessman who had been brought to hear Dr. Graham by a friend. All rejoiced when they saw him walk forward. A chapel member was asked to follow up with him. The man did not want to be followed up with—not at all. He thought walking forward saved him. Wrong. In my opinion this man was not converted.

We cannot always know for sure who is saved and who is lost. But one thing is for certain: we are saved by grace, not works. And the heart, not just the head, must be at the bottom of any profession of faith if it is to be valid.

Martin Luther said he expected heaven to have three surprises in store: people will be there he did not expect, some people he expected to see will not be there, and— the greatest surprise—"That I'm there myself."

Dr. Martyn Lloyd-Jones used to say that a Christian is a person who is "surprised" that he or she is a Christian. Moreover, if they are not surprised, he would question whether they were truly converted!

Jacob was thrilled to get a word from God: "Go back to Bethel."

Do you need to return to Bethel? Have you wandered far from God? Do you feel that God has deserted you? Is God calling you back to Bethel?

Bethel is a symbol of hope. It symbolizes the manner

in which God shows up when you feel absolutely nothing. Bethel symbolizes the God who surprises, the God who will never leave us. Many think there is no hope, but there is—there is hope for you.

God is calling you home.

A woman came up to Arthur Blessitt in South America. When she saw him, she said, "I have wanted to find you for years. I came to your coffee shop in Sunset Strip many years ago. You prayed with me. I immediately went to the phone and called my parents to say, "'I'm coming home.'" She went home. She became a missionary to South America.

On the day I first visited Yasser Arafat, as Canon Andrew White, Lyndon Bowring, Alan Bell, and I were walking away from his compound, Arafat was waving good-bye to us. At that moment the sound of the Muslim call to prayer could be heard in ancient Bethel—now Ramallah—from several directions. It was one of the strangest and most memorable moments of my life. I have thought about this many times.

It is my hope that one day the God of Abraham, Isaac, and Jacob will again be the focus at the historic place once known as Bethel. It is my prayer that Muslims—even the Palestinian leaders, some of whom I still pray for daily and who live in Ramallah today—will discover the God of the Bible and will come to know Jesus Christ as the eternal Son of God who died on the cross for all people. It is my prayer that the ancient promise that "the earth will be filled with the knowledge of the glory of the LORD, as the waters cover the seas" will be fulfilled soon—very soon (Hab. 2:14).

When Jacob first prayed when coming to that "certain place" called Bethel, he felt nothing. He only knew that he prayed. But in a few hours he could say, "Surely the Lord is in this place, and I did not know it." He added, "How awesome is this place!" (Gen. 28:16–17).

Jacob's experience shows that when we don't feel God, He is nevertheless here, and it demonstrates the awesomeness of the unconscious presence of God.

CHAPTER 2

When God Hides His Face

Truly You are a God who hides Yourself,
O God of Israel, the Savior.
—Isaiah 45:15

Whom the Lord loves He disciplines, and
scourges every son whom He receives.
—Hebrews 12:6

"GIVE ME THE keys, son," my grandmother said to me. She meant the keys to the 1955 Chevrolet she purchased for me in March 1955. It was now in July 1956—some sixteen months later—and she was taking the car back. She had a complete right to do this. She initially bought this car for me because I needed transportation from Trevecca Nazarene College in Nashville, Tennessee (where I was a student), to the Church of the Nazarene (of which I was the pastor) in Palmer, Tennessee—112 miles away. It was a small church that called me to be their pastor while I remained a student. But I resigned the pastorate on May 20, 1956, approximately fifteen months later. Her demanding the car back was absolutely fair since I was no longer pastor there.

However, there was another reason—the real reason—she took the car back. It became apparent to her that

I would not remain a Nazarene. Had there not been a major theological change in me during the previous fifteen months, she would have had no problem with my keeping the car.

In one sense, giving her the car did not hurt at all. I was absolutely convinced I was following the Holy Spirit. I had a great sense of peace when I gave her the keys. And yet I must say it did hurt a lot—not for losing the car but because I had somehow become convinced that both my grandmother and my father would rejoice in my theological change. But they did not rejoice with me. Far from it. They were totally convinced I had "broken with God," as my dad put it.

Hebrews 12:6

I vividly remember lying on a bed in my grandmother's home, praying one August afternoon in my hometown of Ashland, Kentucky. I was distraught. "Why?" I asked. Nothing was going according to plan—that is, according to what I assumed would happen. For one thing, I was given a clear vision months before—I thought it was from God—which showed that my dad would be pleased with me. The opposite was true. Virtually all my relatives and Nazarene friends disagreed with my new direction. I felt so alone.

As I lay on the bed that August afternoon I heard the words "Hebrews 12:6." I reached for my Bible to see what it said. It read: "For whom the Lord loveth he chasteneth, and scourgeth every son whom he receiveth" (KJV). As far as I can recall, I had never seen that verse before. But it became clear to me that I was being chastened. But for what? Had I displeased the Lord? Was I now out of His will? Was God punishing me through my grandmother taking back the car? Was God chastening me for going against my godly father and grandmother? Could it be that they were right and I was wrong?

Somehow I didn't think so. True, what was now happening before my eyes did not coalesce with my visions that God was going to use me one day—and that my dad would be proud of me. Nothing was adding up, but I still knew I was being obedient to the Lord. I had nothing to go on but the inner testimony of the Holy Spirit—a phrase I would learn years later.

One could say I was being stubborn. One might say I was too proud to admit I was wrong. I could understand it if people thought this. And some did. But I knew in my heart of hearts that God was with me and that I was following Him.

I also was given what I believe was a clear insight as to part of the meaning of *chastening*. I could see that it was an essential part of my preparation for the future. It was my introduction to a teaching that would become a vital part of my entire theology.

Chastening. Most versions of the Bible now translate the Greek word *paideuei* as "disciplining." It is word that I have since come to grasp as "enforced learning." I knew that God was dealing with me as a Father corrects his son. The word *scourge* comes from the Greek word *mastigoō*, which means "whip with thongs"[1]—a pretty painful kind of punishment if you ask me.

But what had I done wrong? Was there any sin in my

21

life that caused God to punish me? I can answer: there was no overt sin in my life. Not the slightest. I was perhaps not unlike Job who was "blameless and upright, fearing God and avoiding evil" (Job 1:1). That was me. Then. But God saw my heart as I didn't see it. And as Job would later see his utter sinfulness and self-righteousness before God (Job 42:6), so was I going to need a process—a long one—that would eventually cause me to see myself with objectivity: a heart that was vile, deceitful, and desperately wicked (Jer. 17:9).

My Nazarene teaching had no concept of sin in the life of a godly believer. Nazarenes taught that one lived "above" sin. And in a sense I did, but I had a lot to learn. Like Job. My introduction to the doctrine of chastening—a painful process that would lead me to see my self-righteousness— was by having my dad and grandmother reject my new path. Losing the car was easy. Not having their approval was torturous for me, and it lasted a long, long time.

That long ordeal led to what is possibly the most salient thrust in my entire preaching and writing ministry for the last sixty years: the theme of vindication. If you were to take all my sermon notes and stick a needle with a blue thread to represent vindication through all relating to it, I suspect you would find that blue thread in almost every sermon. The need to be vindicated went so deep in me during 1956 and the years following that it led me to focus on the hardest thing to learn: vindication is *God's* prerogative, and His alone. It is what He does. You could say it is one of the things He does best. And any attempt on our part to help Him in this only sets the process back. He does not want our help. He does not need our help.

And when we insist on vindicating ourselves—or helping Him—we deprive Him of doing what He wants to do.

Chastening—or the process of being disciplined—is essentially preparation. It means God is not finished with us yet. It is the way God chooses to prepare us for service and make us partakers of His holiness (Heb. 12:10–11). Yes, He can—and does—punish us for doing wrong. He did it to King David after his adultery with Bathsheba and his having her husband, Uriah, killed in battle (2 Sam. 11–12). But we don't need to commit adultery or murder to warrant God's chastening us. He chastens us because of our *potential* to sin. You could call it preventive medicine. His chastening does not guarantee that we will never sin overtly, but it certainly brings us to see what we are like. And the sight is not glorious. God chastens us to humble us, warn us, and bring us to submission to His sovereign will.

That is why God did not allow my dad and grand-mother to rejoice in my new theology and ecclesiastical direction. God used them to get my attention in an area I did not think I needed.

Life-Changing Experience

My life-changing experience began on the Monday morning of October 31, 1955. Those readers who have followed my ministry over the years know already what I am about to tell. I was driving back to Trevecca Nazarene College in Nashville. I had just come to the bottom of Mount Eagle on old US 41. I turned the radio off (I normally would play the radio all the way) because I felt a heavy burden to pray. At first I felt no sense of God. Quite the opposite, I felt so bereft of any assurance that I questioned my relationship with Him—whether I was even saved (not to mention being sanctified wholly as I believed in those days). Two Bible verses came to my mind: "Casting all your care upon him, for he careth for you" (1 Pet. 5:7, KJV), and "My yoke is easy, and my burden is light" (Matt. 11:30, KJV). I agonized that God would help me to cast my care upon Him so I could say, "My yoke is easy, and my burden is light."

All of a sudden, there was Jesus literally, visibly, and personally interceding for me at the right hand of God. He was as real as anybody or anything I had seen in my life. I immediately sensed how *literal* it all was—that Jesus was at the *right hand* of the Father. I could sense the Father behind me; Jesus was at *His* right hand—and to my right as I continued to drive toward Nashville. What moved me most was His love for me. I saw that He cared more about me than I cared about myself. He was fully aware of all that had been on my mind—every concern I had. I burst into tears. I never felt so loved. I stopped praying. I just watched.

The funny thing was, I knew Jesus was interceding for me, but I could not tell what He was saying. I only knew how much He loved me. His intercession carried on *as though* He were putting His life on the line before the Father—as if having to persuade the Father to come to my rescue. I am not claiming to understand this; I am only describing what I clearly felt at the time.

The next thing I remember—an hour later as I drove through a town called Smyrna, Tennessee—I heard Jesus say to the Father, "He wants it." The Father replied, "He can have it." In that moment I felt a sweet relief, a wonderful peace; I would learn to call it the rest of faith. I believed that day and I believe now that it is the very rest described in Hebrews 4:10: "He that is entered into his rest, he also hath ceased from his own works, as God did from his" (KJV). Ceasing from my own works describes how I *felt*; ceasing from my own works furthermore shows that I no longer rely on my own works to know I am saved. That was "it." I could feel warmth in my chest. I immediately thought of John Wesley's heartwarming experience on Aldersgate Street, London, when Wesley was fully assured of being justified by faith. During that time, for a few seconds—less than half a minute—I saw Jesus looking right at me.

Before the end of that day I crossed over into what I would later know as Reformed theology. I knew without any doubt that I was eternally saved. I knew absolutely that Jesus was physically raised from the dead. I was impressed that He is truly a *man*. I knew He was personally coming back again. I also knew that what happened to me was a work of the Holy Spirit. There was nothing I could do to make what happened to me happen to another person. For a short while I thought I may have been the first since the apostle Paul to experience and believe what was becoming real to me. What was *so* thrilling in the months to follow was to learn I had merely come to see the sovereignty of God without having read a single word of John Calvin or a Puritan. I am amazed at this to this very day. There was nothing in my Nazarene background to anticipate such a belief. I was taught the very opposite.

"You're going off into Calvinism," my professor Dr. William M. Greathouse cautioned me.

"What is that?" I asked.

"We don't believe that," he said, referring to teachings such as eternal security of the believer and election.

I looked at him and said, "Then we are wrong."

Within months of that experience I began to have visions. Not dreams, but open visions. Some were literally fulfilled in months, and some in years. For one thing, I saw that my future ministry would be outside my old denomination. Until then I could not conceive of thinking outside the "Nazarene box," as one might put it nowadays. I also had visions that great revival would go around the world, based largely on the message that Jesus is coming soon—and everybody believed it! Those are some of my unfulfilled visions.

Those were amazing days, lasting until mid-1956, when it became apparent that I would lose the approval of my dad and grandmother. I entered into an era of God hiding His face from me for a long period of time.

The word I received while lying on my grandmother's bed when I heard "Hebrews 12:6" not only explained to me what was going on at the time; it was also prophetic. It showed what would be going on for a long time—a very long time.

"Don't Forget Your Nazarene Background"

I need now to say something important to you about my dad, my grandmother, and my old denomination. First, my father. He was the godliest man I ever knew. My earliest memory of him is seeing him on his knees praying for thirty minutes every morning before he went to work. He was not a minister. He was a pastor's dream—the strongest layman (probably) in my old church in Ashland, Kentucky. He loved God, the Bible, his church, and the services. For vacations he would find out where camp meetings were going on so he could sit under anointed preaching. He read his Bible through many times. His prayer list, which he went through every day, included *hundreds* of names and situations. He *so* wanted me to excel in his denomination.

Second, my grandmother—"Mother Kendall," they called her. People would frequently go to her home to ask her to pray for them. Pastors leaned on her prayers. They sought her counsel. Her Bible was underlined from Genesis to Revelation. She loved the Word, worship, and singing. Indeed, she *lived* for God and her church. She wanted me to preach at her funeral one day and even gave me the text she wanted me to use. You can imagine how hurt she was when I took a different theological direction from hers.

Third, my old denomination. You might like to know that one of the things that caused Dr. Martyn Lloyd-Jones to love me as he did and choose me to be his successor at Westminster Chapel was my former denomination. "Don't forget your Nazarene background," he would say to me again and again. "That is what has saved you," he would add, by which he meant it is what saved me from being a "perfectly orthodox, perfectly useless" Calvinist (which he feared typified so many Reformed ministers). "Preach like a Nazarene," he said to me on the day Westminster Chapel officially called me to be its senior pastor.

I should add that through the influence of Dr. William M. Greathouse, Trevecca Nazarene University, as it later came to be called, honored me with a doctor of divinity degree in 2007. I can assure the reader that I treasure my Nazarene background more than words can express.

Three Kinds of Chastening—or Disciplining

In April 1956 I heard a sermon by Dr. Hugh Benner, general superintendent of the Church of the Nazarene, that impacted me deeply, almost too deeply, if that is possible. He preached on Philippians 2:5: "Let this mind be in you all, which was also in Christ Jesus." He made the point that Jesus had become the "lowest possible shame" for the glory of God. Following that sermon I went to my knees. For some reason I asked God, "Make me the lowest possible shame for Your glory." I really did. Perhaps I shouldn't have prayed like that, but I did. At the time I prayed that prayer there seemed no possibility of a prayer like that being answered. I was on top of the world. I was experiencing the happy showing of God's face. When God shows His face, life is wonderful. Thrilling. Sometimes ecstatic. Nothing seems to go wrong. I was pastor of a Nazarene church, student assistant to the dean of religion, Dr. William M. Greathouse (who later became president of Trevecca and general superintendent of the Church of the Nazarene), and considered by some to be the fair-haired boy of my denomination. I had no problems. But in less than three months my family members said to me, "You are a shame, a disgrace."

My bright future suddenly became bleak. My dad asked me to pay rent if I stayed at home. I got a job driving a truck for a dry-cleaning establishment. I eventually left home. I had to buy an old used car for transportation. I then started selling baby equipment. I did not return to Trevecca the following autumn.

In August 1956, following his comment "You have broken with God," my father asked for proof that I had not broken with God. I tried to come up with something. I resorted to one of my visions. I knew that God was going to use me one day, including having an international ministry. When I described one of the visions, he said, "When? When will this be fulfilled?" I replied that it would happen in one year. But a year later I wasn't even in the ministry. Five years later I was a door-to-door vacuum cleaner salesman. My dad felt totally vindicated in his assessment of me.

Hebrews 12:6 is what gave me a sense of sanity. Not even one of my visions pointed to the long era of rejection I experienced. All my visions were positive, indicating wonderful things down the road. But Hebrews 12:6, which came to me supernaturally, is what gave me a reason for living. I had done no wrong (that I knew of) to bring on the chastening of the Lord. But I had a lot of wrong inside me that needed to surface—and be dealt with. Bitterness. Self-righteousness. Anger. Deep hurt. The notion of total forgiveness never entered my mind. There was so much wrong in me those days. I needed a lot of sorting out. I needed every bit of the chastening of the Lord I was experiencing.

Years later I would develop my own teaching of chastening. Chastening is essentially the hiding of God's face. It is when we hit a wall. Nothing makes sense. The same God who was so real and gracious yesterday seems like an enemy today. You pray and heaven seems like brass. You get no answer, no comfort. You feel deserted. It is what David experienced from time to time and what he dreaded most:

> O Lord, do not rebuke me in your anger, nor discipline me in the heat of Your anger.
> —Psalm 6:1

> Why do you stand far off, O Lord? Why do you hide Yourself in times of trouble?
> —Psalm 10:1

> How long, O Lord? Will you forget me for good? How long will you hide your face from me?
> —Psalm 13:1

Oliver Wendell Holmes (1809–1894) expressed the experience this way: "Our midnight is Thy smile withdrawn."[2] John Newton (1725–1807), best known for "Amazing Grace," also wrote a hymn that depicts the hiding of God's face:

> How tedious and tasteless the hours
> When Jesus no longer I see!
> Sweet prospects, sweet birds and sweet flow'rs
> Have all lost their sweetness to me.

The midsummer sun shines but dim,
The fields try in vain to look gay;
But when I am happy in Him
December's as pleasant as May.[3]

There are three kinds of chastening, or disciplining: internal, external, and terminal.

Internal chastening

That is when the Word of God operates on our hearts. It is when we are disciplined by the Word. His Word is sharper than any two-edged sword (Heb. 4:12). All that is in Scripture moreover is God's plan A—to reach us through what He has spoken already.

But internal chastening does not always work. I'm ashamed to say that it did not work entirely with me. All that Jesus taught about forgiveness, loving your enemy, and self-righteousness was in my Bible! I'm sorry, but it did not seem to faze me. I needed help: external chastening.

External chastening

This is God's plan B—when He comes from without. He resorts to other means to get our attention: people rejecting us, financial reverse, sickness, the withholding of vindication, losing a friend. The list is endless as to the ways God may get our attention. Certain Corinthians experienced this: "For this reason many are weak and unhealthy among you" (1 Cor. 11:30). God afflicted them over the way they abused the Lord's Supper.

God used a big fish to swallow Jonah. That is what led Jonah to seek God as he had not done. Jonah was in the belly of the fish for three days and three nights. "*Then* Jonah prayed" (Jon. 2:1, emphasis added).

What will it take to make *you* pray?

Most of us need some form of external chastening. That is what David meant by the hiding of God's face. Martin Luther taught us that we must know God as an enemy before we can know Him as a friend.

"Truly you are a God who hides Yourself, O God of Israel, the Savior" (Isa. 45:15). The irony of God's chastening is that when He seems so *absent*, He is totally *present* with us. The hiding of God's face is His unconscious presence. Never underestimate it. Be thankful for it. It is what we need.

Terminal chastening

This means your time is up. It is the worst scenario imaginable for a Christian. It is carried out in one of two ways—and sometimes both. First, it can be carried out by a premature death. Certain Corinthians experienced it, owing to their abuse of the Lord's Supper: "A number of you have fallen asleep" (1 Cor. 11:30, NIV). God took them home. They were saved: "When we are judged, we are disciplined by the Lord, so that we would not be condemned with the world" (v. 32). It is similar to the "sin that leads to death" (1 John 5:16). It is my opinion that this happened to Ananias and Sapphira. They were true believers, but greed crept in. They consciously lied to the apostles—and consequently to the Holy Spirit—and were struck dead on the spot (Acts 5:1–11).

Second, terminal chastening may be carried out by one's utter inability to be renewed to repentance in this life. Such a person lives on but never again tastes the joy of being changed from glory to glory. Those described in Hebrews 6:4–6 were saved people who had become stone deaf to the voice of the Holy Spirit; they could not be renewed again to repentance. I am quite sure I have personally seen people like this. As for those who experience both kinds of terminal chastening, I would put King Saul in this category. He lived for some twenty years in a condition of being unreachable and then came to a horrible end (1 Sam. 31).[4]

Why Does God Hide His Face from Us?

We can find significant truths in Hebrews 12:1–11 on God's chastening; indeed, this is one of the most encouraging sections in the New Testament. The writer had just written about the great men and women of faith in Hebrews 11. He then encouraged his readers to follow in the steps of these people of whom the world was "not worthy" (v. 38): "Since we are encompassed with such a great cloud of witnesses, let us also lay aside every weight and the sin that so easily entangles us, and let us run with endurance the race that is set before us" (Heb. 12:1). He points out that these Hebrew Christians had not yet shed blood—died by the sword—for their faith, then reminds them of the ancient word that addresses them as sons: "My son, do not despise the discipline from the Lord, nor grow weary when you are rebuked by Him; for whom the Lord loves He disciplines, and scourges every son whom He receives" (Heb. 12:5–6).

You will recall that this includes the verse that was given

to me when lying on my grandmother's bed. What truths can we learn from this section in Hebrews? We have seen up to now that chastening is essentially preparation; it is what prepares us for future service, showing that God is not finished with us. But what else might we learn?

It is proof that God loves us.

God only disciplines those He loves. As I said above, I never felt so loved as I did on that Monday morning on October 31, 1955. That was what I consciously *felt*. But when my grandmother took the car back from me, I did not *feel* so loved. God, however, chose this time to show me in His Word that He loved me. It is one thing to feel His conscious love by His presence, but it's quite another when He tells us only in His Word. The question is, will we rejoice in His Word as we do in His conscious presence?

One of the purposes of God's chastening is to teach us how we must believe His Word during the hiding of His face as much as we do when He makes us feel good. Remember, when God shows His face, He is pleasing us. But when we believe His Word—without the sense of His conscious presence—we have a tremendous opportunity to please *Him*.

We should get as much joy in *pleasing Him* as we do when He pleases us. We please Him by believing His Word; it is impossible to please Him without faith (Heb. 11:6). He pleases us when He shows His face, so when He hides His face and tells us in His Word that He loves us—and we accept this—we please Him. This is when we show we want more of Him and want to know His ways

(Exod. 33:13) rather than just to get more from Him—
that is, to get things we want from Him.

What is your answer to this question: Do you want
more *of* God or more *from* God? When you and I can
show that we please God by rejoicing in His *Word* when
He hides His face from us, we show that we want more *of*
God; we are therefore responding positively to His discipline in a manner that truly pleases Him.

Here's another question: Which gives you more
satisfaction—knowing that you are pleasing Him or
having Him please you?

I love the feeling of waking up after a good night's
sleep. Turning to God in my quiet time when I have had
a full night's uninterrupted sleep becomes a real pleasure,
even more so when I happen to get an extra hour of sleep!
But it just so happened that on this very morning I woke
up an hour early. I was so disappointed. I needed today
to work on this book and wanted a full night's sleep. I
could not go back to sleep. I pleaded with God to give
me another hour—or at least a half hour. I stayed awake.
I finally got up and turned to the Lord, as I try to do
at the very beginning of each day. I was so tired. But I
have this satisfaction: I know I can please Him by praying
as long, as faithfully, and as best as I can anyway. Paul
said we should be "ready in season and out of season"
(2 Tim. 4:2). That means to be equally faithful and dili-
gent whether we feel like it or not. "In season" no doubt
may refer to the conscious presence of God—when it
is relatively easy to pray or to do the work of the Lord,
but "in season" can also refer to feeling good physically. I
therefore want to please the Lord by faithful prayer when

I don't feel so good. I am chuffed knowing that *He* is pleased with me, especially when I don't feel so well. One of the most important verses in the New Testament refers to Enoch, who had this commendation, that he "pleased God" (Heb. 11:5).

I urge you to get your joy by knowing you please Him.

I don't want to be unfair, but consider this: the desire for the conscious presence of God could in some cases be an unconscious wish to avoid faith. Yes. Having to exercise faith is not fun sometimes. There are times we must *choose to believe.* God can pour out His Spirit on us so powerfully that faith is elevated without any struggle on our part, but when God hides His face, we often struggle to believe Him. Therefore sometimes people opt for seeing the miraculous to avoid faith. I repeat, when God manifests His conscious presence, He pleases us. But when He hides His face and we still choose to believe Him, we please Him.

Please do not misunderstand this, but in the hours immediately following my previously mentioned entrance into God's rest, I barely needed faith! *God was so real.* And—oh!—did He ever please me that day. But there came a time down the road when I hit a wall and—oh!—I felt He betrayed me. The truth is, that era of extreme inner joy lasted for about ten months. It suddenly ended. I came eventually to see that the end of that blissful era was introduced by the invitation to please God. He pleased me for a good while. Now I must please Him by accepting the hiding of God's face. That is when "Hebrews 12:6" was given to me. It is what held me from then on.

Chastening is both painful and inevitable if we are truly God's children.

"Endure discipline," the writer says (Heb. 12:7). He acknowledges furthermore that it is "grievous" (v. 11). This means it is likely to last a while. This is why he says we must *endure*. How long? As long as necessary. As every son or daughter is disciplined by their parents, so our heavenly Father disciplines us. Indeed, as long as we need correction. The correcting process is not fun. It is what gets our attention.

Our heavenly Father gets no pleasure in disciplining us. He does what He knows is necessary. My own father used to say, when punishing me, "Son, this hurts me more than it hurts you." I didn't really believe him until my wife and I had children of our own! No good parent relishes having to punish his or her children. It is out of sheer love for them that good parents correct their children. This is what Dr. James Dobson calls "tough love."

Do *all* of us need chastening? Are there some who don't need this disciplining? The answer: we all need it because we are all sinners. "If we say that we have no sin, we deceive ourselves, and the truth is not in us" (1 John 1:8). "The heart is more deceitful than all things and desperately wicked; who can understand it?" (Jer. 17:9). Parents need to discipline their children because "even from birth the wicked go astray; from the womb they are wayward, spreading lies" (Ps. 58:3, NIV). Our heavenly Father disciplines us because we need it. The same God who sees the end from the beginning also sees the potential sin in us—as He did with Job. Not a single person who ever lived could withstand the pressures Job faced—who was as perfect as can be (Job 1:1)—without spewing out shameful self-righteousness. For that reason God keeps us under His loving hand, inviting us to endure hardness lest we take ourselves too seriously.

Not being chastened means that one is not a true child of God.

"If you are without discipline, of which everyone has partaken, then you are illegitimate children and not sons" (Heb. 12:8). God does not discipline those who are not His.

This teaching is also helpful for people who lack assurance of their own salvation. I have dealt with hundreds of people over the years who fear they are not truly saved. I often ask them: Have you ever been disciplined by the Lord? Have you ever experienced His chastening? If the reply is, "I certainly have," I say to them, "This should encourage you; God does not chasten those who are not His own."

Many years ago when our family lived in Fort Lauderdale, Florida, we had a beautiful orchid tree in our front yard. One day I looked out in the yard and noticed that all the flowers—even buds—had been cut off! I knew our three-year-old son, TR, had done this. I immediately dealt with him. He said, "But Billy [the little boy next door] did it too; why aren't you punishing him?" My reply: "He is not our son. You are."

Chastening not only demonstrates that we are God's sons and daughters; it also shows that we have a future, for chastening is preparation for future usefulness.

Our parents were not perfect; our heavenly Father is perfect.

Our parents disciplined us "as they thought best" (Heb. 12:10, NIV). Six of the most common mistakes parents sometimes make in correcting their children are:

1. They discipline because people are watching them; they don't want to be seen as irresponsible.

2. They punish their children out of anger and frustration.

3. They shout at their kids instead of calmly reasoning with them.

4. They motivate their children to strive for excellence out of fear.

5. They set unrealistic goals for their children to achieve.

6. They don't spend enough time with their children. Children spell *love* T-I-M-E.

Enter our heavenly Father. First, He has nothing to prove—to any of His creation, including the angels. Do you think God looks over His shoulder and consults the angels after He disciplines us and asks them, "How do you think I did?" Unthinkable! Rather, asks Isaiah, "With whom did He take counsel, and who instructed Him?" (Isa. 40:14). Answer: no one.

Second, our heavenly Father never loses His temper when He corrects us. He is at perfect peace in all He says and does. He is described as a God of "peace" (1 Thess. 5:23; 2 Thess. 3:16). This is why we are promised to be kept in "perfect peace" when our minds are fixed on God (Isa. 26:3).

Third, our heavenly Father does not shout at us when He corrects us. He calmly questioned an angry, disobedient Jonah, "Is it right for you to be angry about the plant?" (Jon. 4:9). He spoke to Elijah in a "gentle whisper" (1 Kings 19:12, NIV).

Fourth, our Father removes fear from us when He asks us to do His will. He said to young Jeremiah, "Do not be afraid of their faces. For I am with you to deliver you" (Jer. 1:8).

Fifth, God does not require us to be successful—only faithful to deliver His Word: "Go, and tell this people," he said to Isaiah, "Keep on hearing, but do not understand; keep on seeing, but do not perceive" (Isa. 6:9).

Sixth, God always has time for us; He never leaves us or forsakes us (Heb. 13:5). Psalm 139:7 says, "Where shall I go from Your spirit, or where can I flee from Your presence?" "Call to me, and I will answer you, and show you great and mighty things which you do not know" (Jer. 33:3). "I am with you always," said Jesus (Matt. 28:20).

In a word: God disciplines us "for our good" (Heb. 12:10, NIV).

God disciplines us that we "may partake in His holiness" (Heb. 12:10).

All of us are congenitally allergic to holiness. By nature "each of us has turned to his own way" (Isa. 53:6). "They have all turned aside; together they have become worthless; there is no one who does good, no, not one" (Rom. 3:12).

God is holy (Lev. 11:44). He has commanded that we should be holy (1 Pet. 1:16). If only we should embrace with open arms all His commands to be holy—and then manifest holiness! Yes, we have the Holy Spirit. It is the Spirit in us who makes us welcome God's chastening. But the fact remains, we all need some form of disciplining— usually the plan B as I suggested above. God does whatever it takes to get our attention, to drive us to our knees and say yes to His will for us.

It guarantees an intended effect down the road.

You may recall that I said earlier that the Greek word translated "to chasten" may mean enforced learning. At first it is painful, yes, says the writer of Hebrews. "Yet afterward it yields the peaceful fruit of righteousness in those who have been trained by it" (Heb. 12:11). In other words, it's not for nothing! It has a definite purpose. God does not chasten us because He loves to make us sad. He does not want to hurt us. As we discipline our own children to make them better, so God deals with us in a manner that will achieve its intended result.

It tests us and keeps us in our place.

I would add three further intended results from God's hiding His face: first, to test our commitment, and second, to keep us in our place. It is said of Hezekiah, "God left him alone in order to test Hezekiah, to know what was in his heart" (2 Chron. 32:31). Whereas God does not *tempt* us (James 1:13), He certainly may test us. A severe trial makes sin surface in us we had no idea was there. It is embarrassing, as Job found out: "I put my hand over my mouth" (Job 40:4, NIV). Furthermore, God's disciplining us will keep us in our place. Third, He hides His face from us from time to time to keep us from developing an overfamiliarity with Him. When He manifests His conscious presence over a period of time, I am ashamed to admit that I find that I begin unconsciously to develop a feeling of entitlement. I get a bit too familiar with Him. I impute to my relationship an intimacy that is not as strong as I wanted to think. God has a way of humbling us—to keep us from taking ourselves so seriously. Indeed, one of the chief reasons most of us need the chastening of the Lord is to keep us from taking ourselves so seriously.

God Is With Us

There is one major difference, however, between God's chastening His children and our disciplining our own kids. As parents we have to release our children after so many years of watching them grow up. When they come to the teenage years, we have to loosen our grip on them, eventually to give up entirely and trust that the years we had with them will, just maybe, produce solid character. But God never releases *us*. He never gives up. I speak with authority. As I write this, I am eighty-one years old, and I still experience God's chastening. I still discover sin in myself that I did not know was there! I would add this: my tendency to take myself so seriously and to run ahead of the Lord are twin faults that keep God busy in looking after me.

When God hides His face, it is because He is in fact

loving us. In actual fact He never hides His face; He only appears to hide Himself. He is always with us.

My family's rejection of me beginning in 1956 was what I needed at the time. It lasted a long time. My godly grandmother went to her grave in 1972—I did not preach at her funeral—still utterly disappointed in me. But there is a happier ending with my father. In 1978—a year after I had become the minister of Westminster Chapel—my dad changed his tune. As the train was coming into the British rail station at London's King's Cross, he said to me, "Son, I'm proud of you. You were right. I was wrong." I waited a long time—twenty-two years—to hear those words. But they were worth waiting for.

CHAPTER 3

Between the Times

Wait on the LORD; be strong, and may
your heart be stout; wait on the LORD.
—PSALM 27:14

Do not depart from Jerusalem, but
wait for the promise of the Father, of
which you have heard from Me.
—ACTS 1:4

WAITING FOR GOD to act—waiting for Him to show up, to step in, intervene, take over, or fulfill His promise—is arguably the most difficult discipline of the Christian life. The commands to *wait on God*—explicitly or implicitly—emerge again and again in Scripture, but also come with the promise of blessing if we do indeed wait and not give up:

> Those who wait upon the LORD shall renew their strength; they shall mount up with wings as eagles, they shall run and not be weary, and they shall walk and not faint.
>
> —ISAIAH 40:31

Those who wait for Me shall not be ashamed.
—ISAIAH 49:23

> For since the beginning of the world men have not
> heard, nor perceived by ear, neither has the eye seen
> a God besides You, who acts for the one who waits
> for Him.
>
> —ISAIAH 64:4

You might ask, "How long must one wait?" My answer: as long as it takes to see why God said for us to wait. His command is for our good. He would not ask us to wait if what He has in mind were not worth waiting for.

When my wife and I first moved to England, we were impressed with how consistently, beautifully, and without complaining the Brits would stand in a queue. We Americans aren't good at this, and sadly we show it sometimes when in England and jump queues. It doesn't help our reputation!

It is one thing to wait in a queue for an hour or two. But what if God makes us wait in a queue for years?

When Louise and I married, I was working as a salesman. First, I was selling baby equipment; second, life insurance; and third, vacuum cleaners. In my days of selling vacuum cleaners door-to-door—a period that lasted a total of almost eight years—I used to lie on the floor praying and pleading with the Lord, "How long, how long, how long before You will fulfill Your word to me?" I had an eighteen-month break from selling vacuum cleaners when I was pastor of a little church in Carlisle, Ohio, in 1962 and 1963. But things did not go well there. However, while in Carlisle I felt definitely that God gave me this promise: "Behold, the days come, saith the LORD, that I will perform that good thing which I have promised unto the house of Israel and to the house of Judah" (Jer. 33:14, KJV). I took "that good thing" to refer to promises and visions I received back in 1955 and 1956. They certainly weren't being fulfilled in Carlisle. We returned to Fort Lauderdale, Florida, on January 1, 1964, where I recommenced selling vacuum cleaners until 1968.

When I would read the psalmist's word, "It is time for You, O LORD, to act" (Ps. 119:126), I would think "Yes!" I don't know if the psalmist *knew* that it was time for God to act or if he *felt* it was time for God to act! Many times I have wanted to say, "It is time for You to act, O Lord," but I am not sure I have had His warrant to pray like that! It is certainly the way I have felt countless times.

Two Timely Quotations

Two different statements have been given to me over the years that have been sobering and encouraging. The first came from Dr. Clyde Francisco, my Old Testament professor at Southern Baptist Seminary in Louisville, Kentucky. He used to say, "We all tend to think we don't have enough time. The truth is, God gives all of us enough time." I have thought about that a lot, especially when I think—getting older—I fear I won't have enough time to accomplish what I *thought* I was called to do. This brings me to the second quotation. It comes from Terry Akrill, a godly layman from York, England. He used to say to me, "Time is God's domain." I was sobered by that word. It coheres with Dr. Francisco's word, "God gives all of us enough time." That time is *God's domain* indicates His prerogative regarding the timing of all events in the world—including our personal lives. It is a caution not to try to rush God to get on with our plans!

One of the easiest things in the world to do is to run ahead of the Lord. Is it a sin? Certainly. And yet it is what Joseph and Mary did. The child Jesus—aged twelve—had been with His parents in Jerusalem. When Joseph and Mary headed back for Galilee, they assumed Jesus was with them. He wasn't. Unbeknown to them, Jesus stayed back in Jerusalem. "Supposing Him to be in their company, they went a day's journey" (Luke 2:44). I elaborate on this story in my book *The Sensitivity of the Spirit*. I will say to you right here that I pray every single day—and have done for a good while—that God will somehow keep me from running ahead of Him. I have done this too many times.

The big mistake for many of us—certainly for me—is to *try to make things happen*. We do it partly by running ahead of the Lord. I think that is what Abraham and Sarah did when they decided he should sleep with Sarah's maidservant Hagar (Gen. 16:2–4). They had no children. They were trying to make good the promise that God did indeed give to Abraham—that his offspring would be as the stars of the heavens. This was when he was seventy-five and Sarah sixty-five. Years passed after that without Sarah getting pregnant. She gave up hope and suggested that Abraham sleep with Hagar. He did. Although it was a part of God's sovereign plan, Hagar's giving birth to Ishmael gave great pain to Abraham and Sarah. And to the whole world.

How wonderful it is that "all things work together for good" for those who love God, to them who are the "called according to his purpose" (Rom. 8:28). The fact that all things work together for good does not mean all we did was right at the time. When I left home in 1956 and began work as a salesman, I went deeply into debt. I was so foolish. I bought expensive stereo equipment; I even bought an airplane (a Cessna 120)! I bought a car—a new Edsel. I was then too deep into debt to go into full-time Christian ministry. Going into debt like that was not good. But those years as a salesman taught me how to handle money. (I have not owed *any* money to anyone since 1962.) I learned how to work with people. I learned how to be a businessman. I learned that waiting on God has great reward. Those years were not for nothing. All things have worked together for good.

So with you. Are you waiting for God to act? Have you cried out, "How long?" Take heart. He will show up—never too late, never too early, but always just on time.

Most of life, in fact, is "between the times," to use a phrase I learned from Richard Bewes. Richard says that most of life is taken up in the delaying, "in between times" of waiting. We have times of achievement, yes; but those are not the times of definitive character forming. "It is what you and I do during 'in between' periods that shapes how we are going to turn out."

"The Times"

What exactly are "the times"? The most famous newspapers in the world are *The Times* (London) and *The New York Times*. But by "the times" in this chapter I mean when the presence of God is manifested in a definite and unforgettable way: the flood in Noah's day, God's swearing of an oath to Abraham, the Passover and the crossing of the children of Israel through the Red Sea on dry land, the giving of the Ten Commandments, Israel's crossing of the Jordan into Canaan, the days of Samuel, David's killing Goliath, Elijah's confrontation with the prophets of Baal on Mount Carmel, Jesus's death and resurrection, Pentecost. In church history we have the formation of the Nicene Creed (325), the influence of Athanasius (c. 296–373), the writings of Augustine (354–430), the formation of the Chalcedonian Creed (451), the influence of Martin Luther (1483–1546) and John Calvin (1509–64) that led to the Reformation in the sixteenth century, the Great Awakening (1730–1750), the Cane Ridge Revival (1801), the Welsh Revival (1904–1905), the Azusa Street Revival (1906), and the Toronto Blessing (1994). Between these major events there were of course hundreds of other spectacular events that would qualify as "the times." But generally speaking, most of church history—most of life— is between the times.

Are *you* living between the times? I could predict that you are. Are you waiting for the next major thing to happen in the church and in your life? So am I!

Wait, Worship, Watch

What do you do between the times? What do you do when nothing seems to be happening? Life may be boring. You feel you are accomplishing nothing. You work hard but with no apparent satisfaction. You pray but feel nothing. You do all you know to do to obey and please the Lord, but you feel absolutely nothing has come from it. You seek His face; He hides His face. You feel betrayed by the One you relied on and are seeking to please.

So do you quit? Do you stop praying? Do you sulk? Do you shake your fist at God? Do you retire? Do you take a vacation? Do you do something that shows your frustration or your hurt? During the forty-day period following Jesus's resurrection when He would show up and then disappear, Peter may have been frustrated when he suddenly said, "I am going fishing" (John 21:3). Whether Peter and the disciples who joined him were right or wrong, Jesus shortly appeared to them again (vv. 4–22). Was Peter right or wrong to decide to go fishing? It doesn't matter. The Lord showed up; all worked out for good!

Since most of life occurs between the times, we certainly need to know what to do when nothing of consequence seems to be happening. It has been well over sixty years since I began preaching. Even when I worked as a salesman, I paid to be on the radio, started a small paper called *Redeemer's Witness* (that reached only a handful of people), and preached somewhere most Sundays. But those days were definitely "between the times." If you are between the times as you read these lines, I suggest you wait, worship, and watch.

Wait

Your willingness to wait is partly what shows that you really and truly love God. I can prove it. You will recall that early in this chapter I quoted Isaiah 64:4; it refers to those who wait for God. But in 1 Corinthians 2:9 Paul quotes from this passage in Isaiah but with one interesting difference: "Eye has not seen, nor ear heard, nor has it entered into the heart of man the things which God has prepared for those who *love* Him" (emphasis added). Paul substituted "love" for "wait," which shows that loving God is proved by waiting for Him. There are two kinds of waiting. First, you can be waiting for anything—but you don't know what you are waiting for. You just go on. The waiting could go on and on and on. You have no promise to hold on to. You have set no goal for yourself. Life goes on. You may have nothing to look forward to.

This is not good, because we all need something to look forward to. We need something to live for. Even if you don't have an ultimate expectation down the road, you need to be able to look forward to *time with God* every day. His mercies are "new every morning; great is Your faithfulness" (Lam. 3:23).

I want this book to give you a renewed expectancy. Forget goals down the road for the moment. Consider this very day. Yes. Right now. I pray that you will come into a relationship with God whereby you know for yourself how real His presence is. What God has done for others, He will do for you. He is no respecter of persons. Here is a word for you—you can take this to the bank: "You will seek me and find me when you seek me with all your heart" (Jer. 29:13, NIV). That will give you something to live for!

I guarantee this: God is faithful. He will show up in your life in an undoubted manner. He may put you through a bit of frustration—even suffering—*to test you*. Remember that God left Hezekiah to "test" him and see what was in his heart (2 Chron. 32:31). He has done this with me—more than once! He will do it with you. But take note of another relevant verse: *"After you have suffered a little while*, the God of all grace, who has called us to His eternal glory through Christ Jesus, will restore, support, strengthen, and establish you" (1 Pet. 5:10, emphasis added). The King James Version puts it: after you have suffered a while, He will "settle you." I have found it so. So will you.

What do you do in the meantime? Just *wait*. No one said waiting like this would be easy. Standing in a queue—however long—is not anyone's first choice. When you go to a restaurant and they say the wait will be over an hour, you are disappointed, but you wait if you don't have another good option. Sitting in a doctor's waiting room for two hours is not fun (that is why we are called "patients"). It wasn't fun a few years back when Louise and I sat in the Detroit airport for ten hours because of canceled flights or when she had to sleep on a cot overnight in the Chicago airport due to a late flight arrival owing to bad weather.

I have been what some would call a type A personality from as far back as I can remember. For some reason I have always been excessively driven. I hate arriving late for anything. I hate getting off the highway to get gas and watch all those cars going ahead of me—even when I will be back on the road in less than ten minutes. I hate waiting for anything.

But God says *wait*.

The second kind of waiting is when you have something definite to look forward to. You know you won't have to wait indefinitely. It is good to know that "the doctor *will* be seeing you," "you *will* have a table in the restaurant," "the flight *is* definitely scheduled." So too when you have something that is from the Lord—and you know you have not been deceived.

That is precisely what the disciples had going for them. Jesus told them to stay in Jerusalem. "Do not depart from Jerusalem, but wait for the promise of the Father" (Acts 1:4). They had infallible assurance that something from God was coming. When you have a word like that from God Himself, hang on to it. You will not be deceived.

However, the disciples did not know *when* this would happen. Looking back on the event, they might have figured out in advance that the Feast of Pentecost commemorated the giving of the law of Moses. It would seem reasonable that God would do it on that day. But they did not know at first.

Only 120 waited (Acts 1:15). It is possible that more than 500 of Jesus's followers heard Him say to stay in Jerusalem, for Paul says that more than 500 saw the risen Jesus (1 Cor. 15:6). It is possible that after a few days some of them gave up waiting. Those who initially went to an upstairs room "all joined together in prayer" (Acts 1:14). But even the 120 stopped praying long enough to discuss who should replace Judas Iscariot among the Twelve (vv. 15–26). Whether this was a good thing for them to consider has been debated for two thousand years.

The good thing is, those who waited were rewarded. On the Day of Pentecost, "suddenly a sound like a mighty rushing wind came from heaven, and it filled the whole house where they were sitting" (Acts 2:2). Notice that they weren't kneeling. That shows that posture is not the most important thing when it comes to praying.

The main thing is waiting. God does the rest. We don't need to make things happen. Only God can make things happen. I once asked Carl F. H. Henry if he would do anything differently if he had his life to live over again. He paused and then replied: "I would try to remember that only God can turn the water into wine."

Worship

While we wait, we can worship. The manner in which the 120 waited and worshipped was to pray. That was all they knew to do, although Jesus did not tell them to pray. He told them to *wait*. But praying is what they did. You may be sure they worshipped, being filled with gratitude, adoration, and expectation. For Jesus had just told them to wait for the promise of the Father! They knew they were safe in doing nothing but waiting and worshipping.

As far as I can tell, this is the first time anything like this happened among Jesus's followers. They may have prayed before. Surely they did. But why should they pray when Jesus was always there with them? It is much like what Jesus said in reply to those who wondered why Jesus's disciples did not fast as John the Baptist's disciples did. His reply: "How can the guests of the bridegroom mourn while he is with them? The time will come when the bridegroom will be taken from them; then they will fast" (Matt. 9:15, NIV). The bridegroom was now taken from them. Luke does not tell us that the 120 fasted. They may have. They very possibly did. I doubt food was paramount at that time. They were keen to receive the Father's promise of the Holy Spirit. So while they waited, they worshipped and prayed.

Jesus's disciples had plenty of teaching on this subject. In the Sermon on the Mount Jesus gave them the Lord's Prayer (Matt. 6:9–13). He gave them this same prayer again at a different location, probably on or near the Mount of Olives (Luke 11:2–4). He gave them the parable of the persistent widow, which stresses not giving up on prayer—keep on going (Luke 18:1–8). He said in the Sermon on the Mount: "Ask and it will be given to you; seek and you will find; knock and it will be opened to you. For everyone who asks receives, and he who seeks finds, and to him who knocks, it will be opened" (Matt. 7:7–8). It was a lesson on persistent praying.

The ten days between Jesus's ascension and Pentecost gave them an opportunity to put Jesus's teaching into practice. They were on their own now; they did not have Him to coach them, to correct them, or to say, "Good, that's good—keep it up." They just prayed—constantly. In fact they all "joined together constantly in prayer" (Acts 1:14, NIV). How do you suppose they did it? One person at a time? Did they sit in a circle with one person after another praying? Or could it be that they all prayed aloud simultaneously for those ten days (except when they discussed who should replace Judas)? Who knows for sure? But if I were to guess, I would say they all prayed out loud simultaneously—not particularly listening to the people closest to them but rather interceding with vocal earnestness. That is how it seems to have happened when they prayed some time later as reported in Acts 4:24: "They raised their voices together in prayer to God" (NIV).

The kind of praying that the 120 did was certainly worship. Worship of course includes adoration too—including singing, praise, and thanksgiving. There is no way to know the content of the prayers of the 120, but given the outline and order of the Lord's Prayer—which is God-centered and begins with worship, praise, and adoration, I choose to believe that the 120 were totally worshipping God by praise and petition for those ten days. They may or may not have fasted. They surely found ways to sleep over night, whether they slept in this upper room or went to their homes. They had to go to the bathroom. They had to drink water. They probably ate. But the focus was worship.

I have written an entire book on worship, based on Philippians 3:3: "We...worship by the Spirit of God" (ESV). To what extent the 120 could worship "by" the Spirit is not certain. They certainly had not yet been filled with the Spirit, but they all had a measure of the Spirit or they would not have been followers of Jesus. He taught that no one could come to Him except by the Father's initiative—which meant the Spirit (John 6:44, 65). Jesus "breathed" on the Eleven and said, "Receive the Holy Spirit" (John 20:22). I suspect the Eleven were given a measure of the Spirit at that moment.

While we wait, we can worship. Yes. The best thing you and I can do while we wait for God to act is to worship. This is done by prayer, praise, singing, giving thanks, and reading the Bible. When you believe in your heart that Holy Scripture is inspired by the Holy Spirit—that it not merely contains the word of God but *is* the word of God—and you seek to know His will by reading the Bible, that is worship.

I believe you should read good books. You can learn from them, and God may speak to you through them. But the Bible alone is infallible. You worship God when you read the Bible, knowing that God wrote it (2 Tim. 3:15; 2 Pet. 1:21) and that it is therefore infallible.

Whether the 120 had access to some manuscripts of the Old Testament—or had some scrolls with them in the upper room, who knows? But Peter at least knew the Old Testament very well; it comes out in his sermon on the Day of Pentecost (Acts 2:14–36). It is likely that all 120 were fairly steeped in the Scriptures, or they would not have affirmed Jesus as they did. In any case, we worship God by reading the Scriptures, believing they are His word.

Are you waiting for God to show up? Wouldn't you like to be found praying, praising, and seeking God and reading your Bible at the same moment He pours out His Spirit on you? Then you can identify with Isaiah: "Look, *this is our God* for whom we have waited" (Isa. 25:9, emphasis added). Jesus told us, "It will be good for those servants whose master finds them watching when he comes. Truly I tell you, he will dress himself to serve, will have them recline at the table and will come and *wait on them*" (Luke 12:37, NIV, emphasis added).

The reward for waiting for God—and being ready when He manifests Himself—is that Jesus will wait on us.

Watch

You will have just read, "It will be good for those servants whose master finds them watching when he comes."
This is a word Jesus used with regard to when we are
expecting Him to show up at any moment—including
looking for His second coming: "About that day or hour
no one knows, not even the angels in heaven, nor the
Son, but only the Father. Be on guard! Be alert! You do
not know when that time will come.... Therefore keep
watch.... If he comes suddenly, do not let him find you
sleeping. What I say to you, I say to every one: 'Watch!'"
(Mark 13:32–37, NIV).

The verse I quoted above in Luke 12 regarding "watching"
comes from a parallel passage that does not refer only to
the Second Coming but also to being watchful and listening for the knock on the door. It is a general caution to
all of us to be ready for the Lord to show up at any time:
"Be dressed ready for service and keep your lamps burning,
like servants waiting for their master to return from a
wedding banquet, so that when he comes and knocks they
can immediately open the door for him" (Luke 12:35–36,
NIV). In my book *Prepare Your Heart for the Midnight Cry*
I refer to a Nigerian woman named Grace. She used to
say, "I want to stay close to the door," not too far away to
hear the knock!

Luke 12:35ff therefore also refers to *listening*. You listen
for the knock. To the Laodicean church—a lukewarm,
smug, and wealthy church—Jesus said: "Listen! I stand at
the door and knock. If anyone hears My voice and opens
the door, I will come in and eat with him, and he with
Me" (Rev. 3:20).

Have you been lukewarm in your devotion to Christ? Are you neither hot nor cold? Do you realize Jesus would prefer that you were either hot or cold? If you are lukewarm, he gives you this melancholy promise: He will spit you out of His mouth (Rev. 3:15–16). Here are six sure signs you may know you are neither hot nor cold:

- You don't read your Bible daily but rather now and again.

- You only pray when you have a need; the idea of waiting before Him daily in prayer and worship is not something that has gripped you.

- You complain when a trial comes rather than try to count it pure joy.

- You hold a grudge against an enemy rather than pray for them.

- You are not living in expectancy that God will manifest His presence to you.

- You take your prosperity as the sign that God is with you and is pleased with you.

Count on it, dear reader: I'm sorry, but the Lord Jesus Christ *will* eventually spit you out of His mouth. Then it will be too late. Jesus told this parable:

> The land of a rich man produced plentifully. He thought to himself, "What shall I do, for I have no room to store my crops?"
> Then he said, "This I will do: I will pull down my

barns and build greater ones, and there I will store all my grain and my goods. And I will say to my soul, Soul, you have many goods laid up for many years. Take rest. Eat, drink, and be merry."

But God said to him, "You fool! This night your soul will be required of you."

—Luke 12:16–20

Don't let that happen to you. Make sure you are not lukewarm! May God build a fire under you as you read this book, that it will lead you to be on fire for God!

While we wait, we watch—and listen. Before we can open the door on which Jesus knocks, we must *hear* His voice. Then we can open the door.

This means we must be quiet. We don't want to miss the knock on the door. We must be still. He may choose to speak in a still small voice—a gentle whisper. "Be still, and know that I am God" (Ps. 46:10). John Wesley said we should spend two hours talking to God for every one hour we spend talking with each other. Pastor Richard Wurmbrand said to me almost fifty years ago: "Young man, spend more time talking to God about men than in talking to men about God."

How much do you pray?

We must wait, worship, and watch. We must be still and stay quiet. We don't want to miss the sound of His voice. But this does not mean we cannot walk and pray. It does not mean we cannot jog and pray. I try to walk at least a mile a day on the treadmill. Sometimes I spend this time watching TV, but sometimes I spend the time praying.

Jesus said for us to "watch and pray" (Matt. 26:41). Not

pray and watch. Why this order? If we pray and then watch, we might unwittingly allow a loophole for the devil to get in. I have had people say to me, "I prayed about it, and the next thing I knew I gave in to temptation." This is why Jesus said *watch and pray*. Watching will keep you on your toes. If you have a prior commitment not to make provision for the flesh, you are less likely to give in to temptation. "Put on the Lord Jesus Christ, and make no provision for the flesh to fulfill its lusts" (Rom. 13:14). The best way to avoid falling into sin is to avoid falling into temptation. Most of us have a fairly shrewd idea of what—or who—will tempt us. Don't go there! Don't go near the place, person, or situation where you know in your heart of hearts what will possibly entice you. Whether it be with reference to sex, money, or whatever, avoid going where you are likely to be tempted. This then is why Jesus said, "Watch and pray that you enter not into temptation. The spirit indeed is willing, but the flesh is weak" (Matt. 26:41).

The reward for watching is that you will one day be able to *watch the Lord step in* and take over! Yes. After the sound like the blowing of a violent wind came the privilege of getting to watch: "They *saw* what seemed to be tongues of fire that separated and came to rest on each of them" (Acts 2:3, NIV). What a sight that was. They weren't praying—they were watching! Expectation means watching, or looking for; manifestation of the Spirit means seeing.

While we wait, we watch. The reward for watching is getting to see God work in your behalf. When that happens, you get to become a spectator.

Are you looking for a Christianity that will keep you excited, thrilled, riveted, and buoyant twenty-four hours a day, seven days a week, three hundred sixty-five days a year? Tell me when you find it! And if you think you have found it, I'm sorry; you have not found biblical Christianity. Elizabeth Taylor was married to seven different men—always looking for the perfect husband who would keep her satisfied and happy. Martin Luther said that God uses sex to drive a person to marriage, ambition to drive them to service, fear to lead them to faith. But the physical love that makes people want to get married must make room for *agape* love—unselfish love. It is *agape* love that will sustain a marriage.

We have two grandsons—Toby and Timothy. Both of them want to be entertained constantly; you have to keep them occupied or they get bored and come crying to have something to keep them excited. This of course will have to change as they mature. But I fear many Christians are like children: they want a Christianity that keeps them happy all the time. A vital part of Christian maturity is learning to live between the times. Too many of us pray, "Lord, give me patience—now!"

Hebrews 11—the "faith chapter" of the Bible—is an account of people who accomplished extraordinary things. Hebrews 11 is not about what happened between the times but rather the times of amazing achievement. Read it. Then consider how many years passed *between* the exploits and accomplishments of those great people. The two greatest men in the Old Testament were Abraham and Moses. When Abraham was seventy-five, the Lord told him, "Go from your country, your family, and your father's house to the land that I will show you" (Gen. 12:1). He was promised Canaan for an inheritance, but God gave him "no inheritance here, not even enough ground to set his foot on" (Acts 7:5, NIV). Figure that out! At the age of 85 he had virtually given up on having an heir. He lived to the age of 175. The high-water mark of his life was when God swore an oath to him—perhaps around the age of 110, when he became willing to sacrifice Isaac (Gen. 22:16). Most of Abraham's years were characterized by waiting, challenge, bewilderment, and suffering.

Moses lived to be 120. He thought God would use him when he was 40, but God did not really use him until he was 80. The following forty years were filled with pain and agony—being questioned regarding his wisdom virtually nonstop and misunderstood day and night by his following, the children of Israel. Yes, there were moments when God manifested His glory—the keeping of the Passover, crossing the Red Sea on dry land, the unveiling of the Ten Commandments, and the pillar of fire and cloud. But most of Moses's life was consumed by coping with the extraordinary unbelief of his people.

We all love the times when God clearly shows up—like when He swears an oath to us or enables us, as it were, to cross the Red Sea on dry land.

Yes, most of life is between the times. And yet it is the anticipation of the conscious presence of the Lord that keeps us going. Indeed, such anticipation is what enables us to wait.

When Jesus gave instructions for the disciples to *wait*—and not to leave Jerusalem (Luke 24:49; Acts 1:4)—such waiting was between the times. But in their case they did not have to wait long—only ten days. What if God makes you wait ten years?

It is between the times that we are privileged to know we are pleasing God. We are doing what we are told to do. And that is when character is born and developed.

CHAPTER 4

The Holy Nudge

When he was forty years old, it came to his
heart to visit his brothers, the sons of Israel.
—Acts 7:23

Do all that is in your heart.
—1 Samuel 14:7

It was a stunning night and a pivotal one for Westminster Chapel and my own ministry. Arthur Blessitt, the
man who has carried a twelve-foot cross around the world
and is in the *Guinness Book of World Records* for the lon-
gest walk in history (41,879 miles), came to preach a his-
torical sermon, "Why Do We Need the Cross?" The place
was packed from top to bottom (both galleries filled) with
people standing along the walls. After preaching for just
over an hour, Arthur gave an invitation for people to
confess Jesus Christ as Lord and Savior. Dozens stood.
Nobody expected this. The occasion was not an evange-
listic event but the annual meeting of the Fellowship of
Independent Evangelical Churches (FIEC).

In the vestry, moments before delivering the sermon,
Arthur casually referred to the invitation he would give
at the close of his sermon. I was not prepared for this.
"Arthur, we don't do that here."

"You don't?" Arthur asked incredulously.

I saw the look on his face and said, "Well, if you feel led, go ahead."

He replied, "I can tell you right now, I do."

It was an extraordinary evening. Apart from the surprising number of people who confessed Christ, the place was buzzing with Arthur's message. Even some of those I might have expected to be stilted and negative were saying positive things.

I had to leave the next day for a brief visit to Spain. But for those three days I could only think of one thing. Never in my life had I felt fire in my bones like this. It is what I would call a holy nudge, a phrase I picked up from my old friend Pete Cantrell.

A nudge may come from without—like a gentle prod from an elbow, or from within—when a sense of duty comes into your heart. A holy nudge is characterized by a sense of duty. I felt I must do all in my power to persuade Arthur to stay in London a while and work with us at Westminster Chapel. He was scheduled to preach for us one more time—the final Sunday evening in April 1982. Before the service that night I put to him my burden that he should stay at the chapel for a while before going to his next destination (which happened to be Norway). He had one request: "If I should agree to stay, can I be myself, or are you going to handcuff me?" I assured him he could do whatever he wanted to do. He agreed to stay. He preached six successive Sunday nights, concluding at the end of May. His ministry changed the chapel and me. Never were we to be the same again. It was the most controversial decision I made in our twenty-five years at

Westminster Chapel. See my book *In Pursuit of His Glory* for further details.

P-E-A-C-E

To be in the Lord's presence may lead to a holy nudge from Him, a feeling that you must do something. But is a "nudge" always holy? No. For many years I have shared an acrostic that helps one know if their "nudge" is holy—that is, truly from God. Ask yourself the following five questions. You must be able to answer yes to all five to be sure you are not being led astray:

- *Providential.* Does the door open, or do you have to knock it down? When Arthur said yes, that made it providential. So far, so good.

- *Enemy.* What do you suppose the devil would have you do? The devil would want me to give in to fear of man and not ask Arthur to spend six weeks with us.

- *Authority.* What does the Bible say? Is there anything in Scripture that would prohibit what you feel? Answer: No. Is it biblical? Yes.

- *Confidence.* Does your confidence increase or diminish at the thought of doing this? This is very important, for when you lose confidence, something has gone wrong. Never had I felt such boldness to proceed to invite Arthur to stay with us.

- *Ease.* What do you *honestly feel* in your heart of hearts? This is where integrity must rule. To quote Shakespeare's *Hamlet*: "To thine own self be true." I knew I could never live with myself if I did not do all I could to persuade Arthur to preach for us for those six weeks.

Next to my friend Josif Tson's admonition that I "totally forgive them"—a moment that lies behind my book *Total Forgiveness*—inviting Arthur was the best decision I made during those twenty-five years at Westminster Chapel.

Peace. Paul told us to do what makes for peace (Rom. 14:19). God will never lead us to do what causes us to lose inner peace.

In this chapter we look into one of the most precarious and delicate but important subjects to be examined when it comes to interpreting the presence of the Lord: the issue of *guidance*.

"How do I know the will of the Lord?" is one of the most frequently asked questions I have had asked of me over sixty years of ministry. How many times have we heard people say, "God led me to do this," "The Holy Spirit told me to say this," or "God has given me a word for you."

There have been a good number of times I have for certain felt a "holy nudge" that turned out to be from the Lord. But there have also been times when I have felt a strong nudge to do something that proved to be of the flesh, not the Holy Spirit.

An impression may come into our hearts to do something,

but does that mean it is from God? After all, the heart is deceitful above all things and incurably wicked (Jer. 17:9).

How can we trust what comes into our hearts?

Origins of a Nudge

There are three possible origins of a nudge: the flesh, the devil, and the Holy Spirit. How to know the difference is the big question! All my life I have sought to know when it is the Holy Spirit; when it is only *me* feeling something—the flesh; and when it is Satan giving me an impression. Among the daily petitions on my own prayer list is: "Lord, help me to perceive quickly what is of the flesh, the devil, and the Holy Spirit and to accept only what the Spirit warrants." The fact that I pray that every morning does not guarantee I will be led of the Holy Spirit all day long. This is another reason we should *watch and pray*—in that order—when it comes to guidance.

In other words, we should have a good knowledge of the Bible, a solid theological foundation, and a genuine openness to the immediate and direct witness of the Holy Spirit. That will help us "watch." We must keep our heads screwed on!

"The flakes you have with you always," a good friend of mind always says. There are bubbleheads out there, well-meaning people who fancy they have a hotline to almighty God. If I took all "words of knowledge" or "prophetic words" seriously that have been given to me over the years, I would be mad by now.

I will go further. I happen to know almost all of the high-profile people who have a reputation for being prophetic; some are alive, while some are with the Lord. I have had them prophesy to me a lot. I can tell you, the best of them sometimes get it wrong. Sometimes badly wrong.

You may recall that one of the reasons God hides His face from us is to keep us from developing an overfamiliarity with Him. It is an easy thing to do, especially when we have been used of Him. We begin to fancy we have a "special" relationship with God. This has happened to me when I have felt a strong anointing when preaching. I began to imagine I had "arrived" and would have this anointing from now on. Wrong. The next time I preached, I did so badly that it was utterly embarrassing.

God knows what we need. He hides His face partly to keep us from feeling overly spiritual. A most intriguing verse is, "Do not be excessively righteous, and do not be extremely wise; why should you destroy yourself?" (Eccles. 7:16). Mark it down: when we begin to feel we are one of God's favorites, God will almost certainly show us how much He *really* loves us by whittling us down to nothing.

Have you ever felt overly righteous? Have you ever taken yourself too seriously? Have you thought you were unusually godly or highly spiritual? Have you thought that you loved God more than those around you do?

Peter

Simon Peter thought that way. He was absolutely certain that he loved Jesus more than all the other disciples combined. When Jesus began washing His disciples' feet, Peter thought he would score points with the Lord by saying, "*You* shall never wash *my* feet!," as if to say, "I respect You too much to allow You to lower yourself to little old me." But when Jesus replied, "If I do not wash you, you have no part with Me," Peter quickly came up with another attempt to impress Jesus: "Lord, not my feet only, but also my hands and my head!" (John 13:8–9, emphasis added).

Jesus ignored this pretentious remark. He saw right through Peter all along. Peter went on to say, "I will lay down my life for Your sake" (John 13:37). I am sure Peter meant that. Many of us have said things like that. In a moment of inspiration when the atmosphere is filled with powerful preaching and glorious worship and praise, plus a challenge to follow the Lord to the death, we fall on our knees and raise our hands in surrender. But later when the crunch comes, many of us show we are no different from Peter. Jesus said to him, "Will you lay down your life for My sake? Truly, truly I say to you, the rooster shall not crow until you have denied Me three times" (v. 38). Peter did indeed deny the Lord. It was the worst moment of his life. When he heard the rooster crow, he "broke down and wept" (Mark 14:72, NIV).

Later on, during the forty-day period after Jesus's resurrection when He unexpectedly appeared on the beach, He singled out Peter, asking if Peter loved Him more than others did: "Do you love me more than these?" Peter still thought he did: "Yes, Lord. You know that I love you" (John 21:15, NIV). Peter was still very self-righteous—enough for God to disqualify him indefinitely for usefulness! Nevertheless, God did use him mightily!

You might think that Peter was cured of his self-righteousness after Pentecost. Surely the coming of the Holy Spirit would eradicate such wickedness from his

THE PRESENCE OF GOD

heart. If only! Years later Peter showed cowardice again. He enjoyed fellowship with Gentiles in Antioch. So far so good. But when some influential Jews came there from Jerusalem—after having been with James—Peter "withdrew and separated himself, fearing those who were of the circumcision" (Gal. 2:12). Paul was indignant and rebuked Peter to his face (v. 14).

Do we ever outgrow being self-righteous? I doubt it. It is like the tongue—which no one can tame. If one "does not err in word, he is a perfect man and able also to control the whole body" (James 3:2). But nobody's perfect. Are you perfect? "If we say we have no sin, we deceive ourselves, and the truth is not in us" (1 John 1:8).

I find this so encouraging. If God could use Peter—and He did, mightily—He can use you and me.

If God could use Elijah—and He did, mightily—He can use you and me. In the most revealing moment of his life Elijah regarded himself as being the only man of God worth his salt. "I alone remain a prophet of the LORD" (1 Kings 18:22). Wrong. Horribly wrong. Just a day or two before, Obadiah had taken a hundred prophets and hid them in two caves (v. 4).

Yes, God can use people who have the Elijah complex. But He also sorts them out, as He did Elijah. (See 1 Kings 19:9–18.)

The Heart: Seat of Personality

Both Peter and Elijah felt righteousness in their *hearts*. Self-righteousness is despicable in the sight of God, but it is the last thing we see in ourselves. This is why Job was put through his long ordeal. You could not have convinced Job he was filled with self-righteousness until his "friends" wore him down and the poison that was there all along finally began to spew out like a geyser.

Do you trust your heart? Really? Do you not realize that our hearts can play tricks on us? This is why we have the admonition not to lean on our own *understanding*. "Trust in the LORD with all your heart, and lean not on your own understanding" (Prov. 3:5). Yes, you must trust in the Lord with all your *heart*—that means being totally committed and motivated to relying on Him. But what motivates us can also deceive us.

God deserts us—as we saw with Hezekiah—to test us in order to see what is in our hearts (2 Chron. 32:31). This was not because God was looking for new information about Hezekiah's heart, as if He did not already know. He tests us that we might discover the wickedness of our own hearts. God already knew what was in Hezekiah's heart. God Himself was not waiting to learn something about Hezekiah! His testing was totally for Hezekiah's sake. God already knows what is in us; He deals with us so that we might see the truth about ourselves. Jesus did not entrust Himself to His mesmerized onlookers, for "He knew all men.... He knew what was in man" (John 2:24–25). This is why Jesus was never flattered by the praise of people, and it is also why He is never disillusioned with us. As Gerald Coates, founder of Pioneer Ministries, put it, He never had any illusion about us in the first place. Nothing surprises God.

Are you feeling a nudge to do something? Do you think it is from God? It may be. But what if it is of the flesh—that is, it's your own idea? Or could it be of the devil? Never forget that Satan masquerades as an angel of light (2 Cor. 11:14).

So you trust your heart? Be careful!

Moses, the greatest man who ever lived before Jesus came, needed tutoring in understanding what was a nudge from God. He thought that at age forty his time had come. He felt a nudge in his heart to do something.

Stephen tells us that when Moses was forty years old, "it came to his heart to visit his brothers, the sons of Israel" (Acts 7:23). Moses grew up realizing he was a Hebrew. How did he know? For one thing, he had been circumcised. He knew he was different from the other Egyptian boys. It was sobering for him to come to grips with his true identity. He was also deeply bothered when he saw the way the Hebrews were treated by the Egyptians. He might have dismissed this; he could have repressed his feelings and not let things bother him. But he could not dismiss what he felt in his heart. This is where integrity kicked in.

An interesting but sobering thing about the heart is that it can be the vehicle of integrity or it can be the instrument of deceit. The heart is the "seat of personality," said Dr. Martyn Lloyd-Jones. "As a man thinks in his heart, so is he" (Prov. 23:7). "Set your heart on the right path" (v. 19, NIV). "Guard your heart, for everything you do flows from it" (Prov. 4:23). Conscience—a divine gift given commonly to all—is rooted in the heart. Feelings come from the heart. Motivation is rooted in the heart. Envy too is rooted in the heart. Indeed, said Jesus, "out of the heart proceed evil thoughts, murders, adulteries, sexual immorality, thefts, false witness, blasphemies" (Matt. 15:18). We are commanded to love God with all our heart, soul, mind, and strength (Deut. 6:5; Matt. 22:37).

But how far do you go in trusting your heart? When Proverbs 3:5 says not to rely on our own understanding, it is pointing not only to our limited knowledge but also to the deceitfulness of the heart.

Do you trust your heart?

When Proverbs says for us to "guard" the heart, it shows that a part of us—call it the mind or will—can rise above the heart and gain some measure of objectivity about ourselves. That objectivity will never lead us to let our feelings be the ultimate verdict regarding what is true. Paul vulnerably revealed this when he said, "My conscience is clear, but that does not make me innocent" (1 Cor. 4:4, NIV). It is *the Lord* who judges us. When God ultimately steps in, "he will bring to light what is hidden in darkness and will expose the motives of the heart" (v. 5, NIV). That is why Paul said he did not even judge himself! We are not qualified to give the infallible verdict—which God alone will give—regarding our various opinions.

Jeremiah 17:9

So what do you do when you feel something in your heart? Can you trust it? The answer is that you must be very, very careful. You may be right. You could be wrong.

Jeremiah, a godly man who stood alone in his day and was even accused of treason by his fellow Jews, knew not to trust his heart. Take a look at various translations of Jeremiah 17:9:

The heart is more deceitful than all things and desperately wicked; who can understand it?

The heart is deceitful above all things, and desperately wicked: who can know it? (KJV)

The heart is deceitful above all things and beyond cure. Who can understand it? (NIV)

The human heart is the most deceitful of all things, and desperately wicked. Who really knows how bad it is? (NLT)

How did Jeremiah know he had gotten it right? That is not an easy question for us to answer. *We* know he got it right because history and Scripture vindicate him. But why was he so willing at the time to stand alone? For one thing, Jeremiah was willing to go to the stake for what he prophesied—and virtually did.

So let me ask you: Would you go to the stake for a "nudge" you feel? I don't want to be unfair, but if you would not go to the stake for what you feel, you should seriously question whether your nudge has its origin in the Holy Spirit.

Moses

Moses waited until he was forty before he came to terms with his true identity. He could then wait no longer. It came into his heart to visit his brothers, the children of Israel (Acts 7:23). Did God put that nudge there? Yes. But does it follow that all Moses did after that was under the direct leadership of the Holy Spirit? No.

What was Moses thinking when it came into his heart to visit his true flesh and blood? Did he fancy himself to be their hero? Was he expecting them to cheer, jump up and down, and thank God that at long last a deliverer had come to set them free? Had he hoped that leaving the palace of Pharaoh and mixing with the Hebrews would make them almost bow and worship at his feet? After all, it was not something he had to do; he was sitting on top of the world—the son of Pharaoh, living in luxury and security. He could have lived like that forever. Was he hoping to demonstrate how gracious he was?

Here is what actually happened. He went one day to where the Israelites were working. The Pharaoh had made their lives bitter, "ruthlessly" making them work as slaves (Exod. 1:14, NIV). Moses looked on their burdens and suffering. He saw an Egyptian mistreating a Hebrew, one of his people. Moses looked in every direction, not wanting to be seen. And then he killed the Egyptian (Exod. 2:12). He did it in secret—or so he thought.

What had come into his heart turned out to be a disaster.

He visited the Hebrews the next day. This time he saw two Hebrews vehemently arguing with each other. Moses said to the man in the wrong, "Why do you strike your companion?" The reply to Moses was, "Who made you a prince and a judge over us? Do you mean to kill me as you killed the Egyptian?" (Exod. 2:13–14).

Oh dear. Moses was shaken rigid. He realized his murder of the Egyptian the day before was known (Exod. 2:14). This was not a scenario he was counting on. His greatest fear was that the word would reach the palace.

It did, and it made Pharaoh his enemy. He could never return to the palace again. From that day on, Moses was on the run.

So what was Moses thinking when it came to his heart to visit his brothers? Stephen tells us: Moses thought his people "would understand that God would deliver them by his hand, but they did not" (Acts 7:25). As the King James Version puts it, "He supposed that his brethren would have understood how that God by his hand would deliver them: but they understood not." Moses was so sure they would.

All this happened because of a nudge Moses felt. Was it a holy nudge? Was Moses led by the Spirit to do what he did? Certainly. But things did not turn out as Moses expected.

The mystery of providence

Could there have been another reason Moses visited his people? Yes. The writer of Hebrews provides an answer: Moses was looking for his reward down the road. What came to his heart, then, was a motivation we don't learn from the account in Exodus. But the writer of Hebrews sheds light on Moses's motive: "By faith Moses, when he was grown up, refused to be called the son of Pharaoh's daughter, choosing rather to be mistreated with the people of God than to enjoy the fleeting pleasures of sin. He considered the reproach of Christ greater wealth than the treasures of Egypt, for he was looking to the reward" (Heb. 11:24–26, ESV).

Moses chose to be ruled by integrity. He was willing to lose everything—which meant he could not lose! He knew he would win, that down the road he would never be sorry.

Did Moses jump the gun by killing the Egyptian? Certainly. But the holy nudge to visit his people was at the bottom of all that would happen afterward. Not all he did was holy. But part of the mystery of God's providence is that what God *permitted* was His way of leading Moses to an era of preparation he would need. He was already instructed in the wisdom of the Egyptians and was powerful in words and deeds (Acts 7:22). So at the natural level he may have been quite ready to lead the Israelites. But he would need more than the wisdom of the Egyptians and to be good with words and deeds. He needed spiritual preparation. He needed to be enrolled in the University of the Holy Spirit. The curriculum called for forty years of a different kind of learning.

Eighteenth-century hymnist William Cowper expressed God's mysterious ways well in a hymn titled "God Moves in a Mysterious Way."

> God moves in a mysterious way
> His wonders to perform;
> He plants His footsteps in the sea
> And rides upon the storm.
> Deep in unfathomable mines
> Of never-failing skill
> He treasures up His bright designs
> And works His sov'reign will.

Jonathan

Another example of a holy nudge at work was when Jonathan, son of King Saul, was gripped by a conviction he could defeat the Philistines. The people of Israel were living in a time of great trouble. In humiliation they had "hid themselves in caves, in hollows, among rocks, and in cellars and cisterns." The people followed King Saul with "trembling" (1 Sam. 13:6–7).

Jonathan refused to be intimidated. An idea came into his heart, and without telling his father, he said to his armor bearer, "Come, and let us cross over to the Philistine garrison which is on the other side.... let us cross over to the garrison of these uncircumcised. Perhaps the LORD will work for us. For the LORD is not limited to save by many or by few." His armor bearer replied, "Do all that is in your heart" (1 Sam. 14:1, 6–7). Jonathan put a fleece out, as it were. "We will cross over to these men, and we will reveal ourselves to them. If they say to us, 'Wait until we come to you,' then we will stand still in our place, and we will not go up to them. But if they say, 'Come up to us,' then we will go up, for the LORD has delivered them into our hand, and this will be a sign to us" (vv. 8–10).

The plan worked. Both Jonathan and his armor bearer showed themselves to the Philistine outpost. The Philistines said, "Look, the Hebrews are coming out of the caves where they have hidden themselves" (1 Sam. 14:11). The men at the outpost shouted to Jonathan and his armor bearer, "Come up to us, and we will teach you something" (v. 12). This is the exact sign Jonathan hoped for. Jonathan said to his armor bearer, "Come up after me. For the

LORD has delivered them into the hand of Israel" (v. 12). Jonathan climbed up to them with his armor bearer, and the Philistines fell before them; they killed about twenty men. "There was trembling in the camp, in the field, and among all the people. The garrison and the raiders also trembled, and the ground quaked. It was the fear of God" (v. 15). Then King Saul and all his men assembled and went into the battle. They found the Philistines in "very great confusion," striking one another with their swords (v. 20). In a word, "the LORD saved Israel that day" (v. 23).

It all begin with a holy nudge: Jonathan's heart conviction that God would give them that victory.

Does God give holy nudges today? Sometimes. Perhaps not every day. We must be guarded. Never forget that the heart is deceitful and incurably wicked. We are fools if we forget this, especially if we may have had a string of successes with following our "nudges."

A Holy Nudge, an Unholy Nudge, and a Holy Nudge

Rabbi Sir David Rosen and I wrote a book together titled *The Christian and the Pharisee*. The book was born one morning when—just moments before breakfast in my quiet time—I felt a nudge to ask David to write a book with me comprised of our letters to each other. I had met David through the Alexandria Process, led by former archbishop of Canterbury Lord Carey, Canon Andrew White, and former president of Israel Shimon Peres. David and I were scheduled to have breakfast one morning at the Mount Zion Hotel in Jerusalem. So at this breakfast I suggested the book: I would present the biblical case for Jesus being Israel's Messiah, and he could reply as he wished. I initially said to him, "Don't answer now—just think about it." But he immediately said, "Let's do it." We did. Although not a best seller as I had hoped, it was published on both sides of the Atlantic. Jewish Christians have widely welcomed it, but I had fondly hoped this book might lead to some Jewish people being saved. So far as I know, that hasn't happened. But as Yogi Berra would say, "It ain't over till it's over."[1] David and I have remained good friends to this day.

This book began with a holy nudge. However, after this book was published, I had another nudge—a huge nudge that turned out to be an unholy nudge. It was precipitated by certain reviewers of *The Christian and the Pharisee* who suggested we write a book that would include Muslims. Yes, I agreed. It came into my heart to write a book on the theme of who has the right to Jerusalem—the Jews, the Christians, or the Palestinians. David agreed to represent the Jews. I would present the Christian perspective, but only after letting all the church leaders in Jerusalem have their input. I asked Dr. Saeb Erekat, the respected Palestinian peace negotiator with Israel, to present the Muslim perspective. He said no but that he would consider writing the foreword to the book. I spent time interviewing or seeking to interview heads of churches in Jerusalem, including Russian Orthodox, Syrian Orthodox, Armenian Orthodox, Greek Orthodox, Anglican, and Roman Catholic leaders. Meanwhile, I learned a lot. All roads led to Egypt if I wanted to get the most powerful Muslim leaders to participate. I was in touch with several people with influence. Things seemed so providential at first. I even went to Cairo thinking the way was prepared for me to meet the Grand Mufti of Egypt. But I hit a wall. Although I would sometimes initially receive encouragement, *all* of them ended up saying no.

I had to admit in the end that my nudge was not from God. I'm afraid I had only a grandiose idea that made sense at the time.

Someone might say, "But surely you were led to write the book; it was they who stopped it." That could be true. But I also had to admit that none of the interviews with the church leaders in Jerusalem flowed. I spent a lot of time and money; I learned a lot and the venture probably did no harm. But I eventually knew in my heart I was pushing for something that God was not in. Yet in the meantime I kept trying until the Muslim leaders who initially said yes, one by one, backed down. In the end I never found any high-profile Muslim leader who would have a part in the book. There is one more factor. I took John Paul Jackson, speaker and minister, with me when I interviewed some of these people. He warned me, "Your ego will drive you to politics. The Spirit will keep you focused on salvation." I have taken that to mean I should stay out of politics not only with Middle Eastern affairs but at home as well. I am thankful that my "nudge" did not result in my writing that book.

What was the difference between the "feel" in my nudge to write *The Christian and the Pharisee* with Rabbi Rosen and my nudge to do a second book, this time with him and a Muslim leader? I could *feel* no difference at first. This is why we must test our feelings. Recall the PEACE acrostic at the beginning of this chapter. The answer as to whether our nudge is truly from God will be made clear when we don't have to knock doors down to make things happen and the nudge leads to peace.

Major Turning Point in Our Lives

I totally understand if you struggle to accept what I now share. I will merely describe what happened to us many years ago. In June 1970, sitting next to my wife, Louise, at a Southern Baptist Convention meeting in Denver, Colorado, I suddenly felt a strong nudge to open my little New Testament for a confirmation of a leading I was feeling. After days and weeks—even years—of reflecting on not having finished my degree at Trevecca, things came to a head: I must decide now to finish or forget it forever. I had this dilemma: I was almost thirty-five—a rather old age for one with a family to return to school—and I was very happy in my church at Fort Lauderdale. But I was not at peace in not having academic credentials, as most ministers had. Was I to give up my church and finish my college degree and then go to seminary? It meant taking some five years out of the full-time ministry, I assumed; moreover, I would not be back into full-time ministry until I was forty. I kept thinking about the age of forty and waiting five years before I would be back in full-time ministry. But did I really want to wait until I was forty for this?

There is more: I knew the gospel, I was experienced in speaking, and I was fairly knowledgeable in the Word of God. Why did I need more education? What could I learn that I really needed? Also, I was settled in my Baptist church in Fort Lauderdale. I was secure. But I wondered what I might feel when I was forty. Would I be glad at the age of forty that I went back to school? Almost certainly, I said to myself. But I needed a clear word from the Lord to move from Fort Lauderdale to Nashville (to get my AB at Trevecca)—and then to move to Louisville, Kentucky, to attend Southern Baptist Theological Seminary (to get the MDiv)—and then to Britain, which was what I aspired to do most of all.

This was so major. I kept thinking, "If only God would give me a word." He had done this at critical times before. Would He be pleased to do it again?

The nudge to open my little New Testament intensified. I have to tell you, opening your Bible to get a verse for guidance is a precarious thing to do. I do *not* recommend it. But that day I decided to follow through with my nudge. However, I asked the Lord for one thing—namely, that what my eyes fell on would be specific, clear, and decisive. With my heart pounding in my chest—I somehow knew our future was about to be revealed—I opened my little King James Version New Testament. My eyes immediately fell on these words: "And Moses was learned in all the wisdom of the Egyptians, and was mighty in words and in deeds. And when he was full forty years old, it came into his heart to visit his brethren the children of Israel" (Acts 7:22–23, KJV). These words could not have been more relevant to what was burning on my heart; everything fell into place. To use a word I would later discover in Britain: I was gobsmacked.

I turned to Louise and explained what just happened.

We agreed together that we would be resigning our church and I would be going back to school. We never looked back.

CHAPTER 5

Questioned Leadership of the Holy Spirit

Led by the Spirit, he [Simeon] came into the temple.
—LUKE 2:27

They [Paul and others] went through the region of Phrygia and Galatia, having been forbidden by the Holy Spirit to speak the word in Asia. And when they had come up to Mysia, they attempted to go into Bithynia, but the Spirit of Jesus did not allow them.
—ACTS 16:6–7, ESV

Now, compelled by the Spirit, I [Paul] am going to Jerusalem, not knowing what shall befall me there, except that the Holy Spirit testifies to me in every city that imprisonment and afflictions await me.
—ACTS 20:22–23

They [disciples] told Paul through the Spirit not to go up to Jerusalem.
—ACTS 21:4

THE PRESENCE OF the Lord and the Holy Spirit are the same thing. And yet we have seen that people do not always sense His presence even when He is present. The sense of God's presence is His conscious presence, and it is this sense that we long for. The sense of God's presence can be manifested in a "holy nudge," which is what I felt when I decided I would ask David Rosen to write a book with me. It is also what I thought I felt when I wanted to write the second book on Jerusalem.

What is the difference between a holy nudge and the undoubted leading of the Holy Spirit? They are the same objectively, but they are not necessarily the same subjectively. Objectivity refers to *fact*; the subjective refers to *feeling*, or our perception. Many factors may be involved when it comes to one's perception of God's leading. We must be able to differentiate between what we want or hope to be true from what the Spirit is truly saying. The Spirit may be speaking clearly, but if our minds are made up, we may well miss what He is saying. Therefore the subjective must always give way to the objective if we are going to arrive at the truth.

For example, subjectively I felt led to write the previously mentioned book on Jerusalem. But objectively I was obliged to conclude that I was not led by the Spirit. How do I know? Things did not work out. I began to lose peace about it. I had to give it up and admit I had gotten it wrong by thinking I was led to write the second book.

Being objective is sometimes extremely hard, especially when we have a strong feeling or opinion about something. We naturally want to believe our opinion is correct. The problem, almost always, is our pride. But getting to the truth requires that we are impartial, neutral, even-handed, and detached from our ego. It may mean asking for and accepting critical input from others. It means we must be *willing* to be seen as wrong. That is so humbling.

Question: Do you want the presence of the Lord so much that you are willing to admit when you get things wrong? How important is the true presence of the Lord to you? Do you want His honor or your personal vindication?

This book is not only about the presence of the Lord but also about the things that can come to us when we are in His presence. I want this book to inspire you to want His presence more than anything in the world. But sooner or later we will have to ask whether our ego need is more important to us than the objective presence of the Lord. In other words, do we want the praise that comes from people or the reward and praise that comes from our heavenly Father? Jesus asked the Jews who didn't believe in Him, "How *can* you believe, who receive glory from another and do not seek the glory that comes from the only God?" (John 5:44, emphasis added).

The four biblical passages that head this chapter, all written by Luke, point to the leadership of the Holy Spirit. But a question might be raised about the Holy Spirit regarding each of these passages.

Luke 2:27

The first Lukan passage has the example of Simeon being led by the Holy Spirit. "The Holy Spirit was upon him. It was revealed to him by the Holy Spirit that he would not die before he had seen the Lord's Christ" (Luke 2:25–26), that is, the Messiah. We don't know how old Simeon was, but he was possibly an old man. This account has led a number of sincere Christians to believe they would not die before Jesus's second coming. In other words, as Simeon felt He would see Israel's Messiah before he died, there are those who believe they will not die but be alive at the time of Jesus's second coming. Simeon is their inspiration for this kind of expectancy. However, I have to say that of those I know about who thought this, all are in heaven today. They were wrong. This goes to show how people can sincerely believe they are hearing from God when they obviously aren't. These people believed they would be alive at the Second Coming because it is what they *wanted*.

Their erroneous thinking shows how we must learn to make a distinction between what we eagerly want and hope is true and the objective word of the Lord. I have been wrong many times. When I was seventeen, I thought the Holy Spirit revealed to me that my mother, aged forty-three, would not die when she became seriously ill. She died two months later. I was absolutely sure I would marry a blonde. Louise has brown hair. I was convinced I would be called to pastor a church in Hallandale Beach, Florida. They called someone else. I could go on and on. All these disappointments were not rooted in the objective voice of the Holy Spirit but in my own wishes.

Luke says several things about Simeon. He was a righteous and devout man who was waiting for the consolation of Israel. This means he wanted to see the fulfillment of prophecy concerning Israel's Messiah to be fulfilled. The Holy Spirit was on him, and one day Simeon was "led by the Spirit" to the temple (Luke 2:27). What is more, he got it right. He really was moved by the Spirit to go to the temple and see the Messiah with his own eyes before he died.

Some people have questioned how a person could experience the immediate and direct presence of the Holy Spirit before the Day of Pentecost. The answer is that the Holy Spirit is as eternal as the Son is eternal and the Father is eternal. But John's statement that the Holy Spirit "had not been given" (John 7:39, ESV)—referring to the era before Pentecost—has led some to ask this question. Concluding to what extent people experienced the Spirit before Pentecost would be speculative, but some certainly did experience the Holy Spirit to some degree, and perhaps to a great degree.

Luke says the Holy Spirit was on Simeon and that Simeon was "led by the Spirit" to go to the temple. This implies that Simeon consciously felt led to go to the temple. It is not likely that Simeon would use language such as "led by the Spirit." I doubt that the term *Holy Spirit* was in Simeon's vocabulary. The Holy Spirit came down at Pentecost more than thirty years later. When Simeon took the child Jesus in his arms, he said, "Lord, now let Your servant depart in peace, according to Your word; for my eyes have seen Your salvation which You have prepared in the sight of all people, a light for revelation to the Gentiles, and the glory of Your people Israel" (Luke 2:29–32). Simeon now knew for sure he had not been deceived!

This proves that the Holy Spirit was indeed present and active in people before Pentecost. Never think therefore that Pentecost was the first time the Holy Spirit came down from heaven. The Spirit of God was active in creation (Gen. 1:2). David prayed, "Do not take Your Holy Spirit from me" (Ps. 51:11). Jesus said that David spoke "by the Spirit" when David wrote Psalm 110:1 (Matt. 22:43). This is because the third person of the Trinity is *eternal*. The writer of Hebrews explicitly calls Him the "eternal Spirit" (Heb. 9:14). He had no beginning and has no end. The writer of Hebrews is saying that what Jesus did on the cross—fifty days before Pentecost—was carried out by the Holy Spirit. Through the eternal Spirit, Christ offered Himself unblemished to God. Not only that, but also the Holy Spirit was behind all that Moses did in setting up the tabernacle in the wilderness. The entire pattern of the ancient tabernacle is to be explained by the leadership of the Spirit: "The Holy Spirit was signifying through this that the way into the Most Holy Place was not yet revealed, because the first part of the tabernacle was still standing" (v. 8).

Therefore what happened to Simeon should not be surprising. The term *Holy Spirit* therefore may not have been in Simeon's vocabulary, but it was certainly in Luke's vocabulary. Writing under the infallible inspiration of the Holy Spirit, then, Luke says that the explanation for Simeon going to the temple when he did was because he was moved by the Spirit to do so.

The inspiration of the Holy Scriptures

We must keep in mind an important principle when considering the role of the Holy Spirit in writing the Bible. I believe in the infallible inspiration of the Spirit when it comes to the reliability, trustworthiness, and authenticity of the Bible. For example, it is one thing for a writer himself to claim something as coming from the Holy Spirit; it is another if he quotes an individual as claiming something from the Spirit, as we will see below. In the case of Simeon, Luke is writing his theological explanation on what lay behind Simeon coming to the temple.

Acts 16:6–7

Acts 16:6–7 presents a difficulty for some. Since Jesus commanded His disciples to go into all the world to preach the gospel (Matt. 28:19; Mark 16:15), how could the Holy Spirit forbid the disciples from preaching the gospel in Asia? If God calls all people everywhere to repent (Acts 17:30), whatever was going on when the disciples were forbidden by the Spirit not to preach the gospel in Asia and Bithynia?

In Acts 16:6–7 Luke clearly says that certain disciples were "forbidden by the Holy Spirit to speak the word in Asia." This incident too apparently reflects Luke's theological opinion. The disciples do not say that *they* perceived this at the time; maybe they did perceive it, but Luke is the one who says it and takes the responsibility for saying it. Because he is writing under divine inspiration, I believe this to be objectively true: *the Spirit prohibited them*. Whether subjectively Paul and others knew from the inner testimony of the Holy Spirit that they were not to proceed or objectively they hit a wall and could not proceed, we do not know. Luke simply says the Holy Spirit forbade them from going further.

I take this passage to refer to what the disciples *felt*, that the Holy Spirit would not give them liberty to proceed where they planned to go. It would mean that God had other plans for them at that time.

One of the more interesting but enigmatic areas of inquiry is to know when it is Satan that hinders or when it is God's providence and the Holy Spirit. For example, Paul says he was hindered by Satan from going to Thessalonica (1 Thess. 2:18). And yet he says that when he was prevented from getting to Rome it was because he was so busy preaching the gospel in other places (Rom. 1:13; 15:20–22).

Like it or not, some things will always remain an enigma. We don't know everything, and we don't need to know everything. And yet in the case of Paul and others planning to go to Asia and Bithynia, Luke clearly attributes the entire situation to the sovereignty of the Holy Spirit. Jesus said that the Holy Spirit is like the wind that blows where it will, and we don't know where it is coming from or where it is going (John 3:8). This may refer to the work of the Spirit in people's hearts, and it can refer to the sovereign providence of God.

That's good enough for me; I believe Luke when he says that they were not allowed by God to proceed. Even if they hit a wall and could not proceed, God is responsible for the disciples not getting to where they initially intended to go. The English Standard Version uses the phrase "Spirit of Jesus" to explain what would not allow them to proceed. This is one of the few times this exact phrase is used in the New Testament. Paul calls Him "the Spirit of God" (Rom. 8:9) and "the Spirit of Jesus Christ" (Phil. 1:19). In any case, the leadership of the Holy Spirit meant that these men could not go to Asia or Bithynia.

We find no hint that the disciples failed in their mission or felt disappointed. Luke clearly attributes the entire scenario to God's sovereignty.

Luke's understanding of God's sovereignty emerges several times in the Book of Acts, although in two places he is only quoting those who believed in it. For example, Peter, in his sermon on the Day of Pentecost, said this about Jesus's crucifixion: "You have taken Him, who was handed over to you by the ordained counsel and foreknowledge of God, and by lawless hands have crucified and killed Him" (Acts 2:23). This verse shows both God's sovereign purpose and also man's responsibility. When the disciples prayed after being threatened, they said those who crucified Jesus did what God's hand and counsel "had foreordained to be done" (Acts 4:28).

Luke does, however, give his theological opinion in at least two places. First, he ascribes the growth of the church in terms of what God did: "The Lord added to the church daily those who were being saved" (Acts 2:47). God was behind the church's growth. Also, when it came to the conversion of the Gentiles, Luke wrote, "When the Gentiles heard this, they were glad and glorified the word of the Lord. And all who were ordained to eternal life believed" (Acts 13:48). Had Luke stated that all who believed were appointed to eternal life, this would have been absolutely true. But Luke was making a theological point: it was those who were appointed—"ordained" (KJV)—who believed. He believed in divine election, that God chose who would believe.

I raised the question of Luke's theology of the sovereignty of God to my Greek teacher in a classroom years ago at Southern Baptist Theological Seminary (this was when the school was very liberal). I pointed out such things as Luke's claim that those "who were ordained to eternal life" were the ones who believed (Acts 13:48), showing divine election. So when I asked the teacher what he made of Acts 13:48, he replied, "I disagree with Luke." He did not question whether Luke was teaching divine election. But he—astonishingly—felt the liberty to rise above Scripture and judge it. I don't have that liberty. I am bound to accept what Luke wrote.

If you were to ask why the disciples were forbidden to speak the word in Asia and why the Spirit of Jesus would not allow them to go to Bithynia, I would have to reply, "I don't know." I would suspect it only meant they were not allowed to go there *at that time* and that God had other plans. The gospel would certainly have come there later! Acts 16:6–7 demonstrates how the early disciples were sovereignly led by the Holy Spirit in all they did—whether by a holy nudge or by hitting a wall.

Acts 20:22 and Acts 21:4

In the third passage Paul is addressing the elders of the church at Ephesus. He refers to his ardent intent to go to Jerusalem and clearly attributes it to the *immediate* leadership of the Holy Spirit. He uses strong language: "And now, compelled by the Spirit, I am going to Jerusalem" (Acts 20:22). The English Standard Version says that Paul was "constrained by the Spirit." In a word, Paul claims that God Himself told him to go to Jerusalem. As an apostle, Paul certainly had the right to make this claim.

But could Paul possibly have confused his own personal determination with the leadership of the Spirit? Could Paul have imputed the Holy Spirit to his personal wish? Could the great apostle Paul have gotten that wrong?

If the Book of Acts ended there—or there were no Acts chapter 21—we would not have a dilemma on our hands. Paul is not trying to prove anything. He is merely updating the elders in Ephesus on what is coming down the road for him. He knows it won't be easy. Luke was present when Paul spoke these things to the elders at Ephesus. What Paul said was straightforward, and all Luke did was report what Paul said—namely, that he was constrained by the Holy Spirit to go to Jerusalem. Luke's report does not mean that he agreed with Paul.

However, what follows in Acts 21:4ff is that Luke quietly challenges Paul's opinion.

Who got it right—Paul or Luke?

We now come to the fourth and most difficult passage I quoted at the beginning of this chapter. Luke says that certain disciples "through the Spirit" urged Paul not to go to Jerusalem (Acts 21:4). This is what makes this passage a problem. Some might say this was an unguarded comment by Luke, or that Luke was graciously affirming the intent of the disciples because they believed they were prophesying by the Holy Spirit. But, surely, either Luke was writing under infallible inspiration or he wasn't. These were prophetic warnings by some disciples at Tyre where Paul stayed seven days. Had not Luke used the words "through the Spirit" in regard to these disciples warning Paul, we would not have an issue before us. We might simply dismiss them as sincere people who felt they should caution Paul. But Luke says they warned Paul "through the Spirit." If this is indeed objectively the case, God was warning Paul. Therefore it is not these disciples but Luke—the author of the Book of Acts writing under inspiration—who says it. They might have been quoted as saying, "Paul, we believe the Spirit has told us you should not go to Jerusalem." Or they might have said, "Paul, we are compelled by the Spirit to tell you that you should not go to Jerusalem." But because Luke says they prophesied "through the Spirit," we have a very important issue before us. And yet Luke does not embellish this statement; he then says, "But when *our* days were over, *we* parted and traveled on" (v. 5, emphasis added). This shows Luke himself was present in all this.

There is more. Paul and Luke continued on their voyage from Tyre, ending up at Caesarea. The "we" passages in Acts indicate when Luke himself was physically present. They stayed at the house of Philip. Luke adds that Philip had "four unmarried daughters, who prophesied" (Acts 21:9, ESV). Luke does not tell exactly what they prophesied, but many scholars suggest that they too prophesied as the previous disciples did, or why else would Luke bother to mention them? Not only that; he then reports the prophecy of Agabus: "Coming to *us*" (that means he came to Luke and Paul), Agabus took Paul's belt, tied his hands and feet with it, and then said, "Thus says the Holy Spirit, 'This is how the Jews at Jerusalem will bind the man who owns this belt and deliver him into the hands of the Gentiles'" (v. 11, ESV). Luke continues, "When *we* heard this, *we* and the people there urged him not to go up to Jerusalem" (v. 12, ESV, emphasis added).

Agree or disagree with Luke, he clearly believes that Paul should not go to Jerusalem. Who are we to believe—Paul or Luke? Did the author of the Book of Acts have more insight on this than the apostle Paul? Or should not Luke have let Paul have the final word? By the way, here was Paul's response to Agabus's prophecy: "What are you doing, weeping and breaking my heart? For I am ready not only to be imprisoned but even to die in Jerusalem for the name of the Lord Jesus" (Acts 21:13, ESV). Paul wrote that we should "not treat prophecies with contempt" (1 Thess. 5:20, NIV) but nonetheless rejected Agabus's prophecy. This is the same Agabus who earlier prophesied a severe famine. The prophecy was fulfilled, says Luke (Acts 11:28). Luke therefore purposefully gave Agabus high credibility. However, when Paul would not be dissuaded by Agabus's prophecy, Luke says, "*We* ceased and said, 'Let the will of the Lord be done'" (Acts 21:14, ESV). Luke, in any case, sided with those who believed that Paul should not go to Jerusalem. One wonders whether Luke's opinion had any effect on his fellowship with Paul in ensuing days. We will find out when we get to heaven!

So when it comes to the knotty question whether the apostle Paul was right to reject the warnings of prophetic people—as he did—the issue is whether Paul could make a mistake in thinking it was the *Spirit* who was behind his determination to go to Jerusalem. Or whether Luke's authority as the inspired writer of the Book of Acts—saying what he did in Acts 21:4—trumps Paul's words in Acts 20:22.

What say you? If you are like many, you assume Paul as an apostle would not have misinterpreted the Holy Spirit.

As one friend of mine said, "I just cannot believe that Paul was wrong."

The Holy Spirit was either for or against Paul going to Jerusalem.

We know two unquestionable things from this account: (1) Luke says that the disciples at Tyre warned Paul "through the Spirit," and (2) Luke sides with those who felt Paul should not go to Jerusalem. The "we" passages confirm this plus the fact that Luke gives so much space to those who oppose Paul: the disciples at Tyre, the daughters of Philip (almost certainly), and the prophecy of Agabus.

Did Paul err? Or was Luke misguided?

So we return to the question, what is the difference between the subjective holy nudge and objectively being led by the Holy Spirit? Paul would claim to have had the holy nudge. But so too would those who disagreed with him!

Could both sides be right? Perhaps. Maybe those who prophesied could see that Paul was going to get in serious trouble in Jerusalem and therefore pleaded with him not to go—except that "through the Spirit" they urged Paul not to go. This tells me that the Holy Spirit was saying, "Don't go." If so, Paul disobeyed. But he probably thought to himself that these people were sincere but were not in touch with the Holy Spirit as he was! We can only be sure that "all things work together for good to those who love God, to those who are called according to His purpose" (Rom. 8:28). But one of the major principles that must govern our thinking about Romans 8:28 is the fact that all things work together for good does not mean that all that happened was right at the time.

Here are ten unquestionable facts. First, Paul did go to Jerusalem. Second, when he got there he was forced to accommodate certain Jews who didn't trust him; he accommodated their worries by taking a vow to prove himself (Acts 21:20–26). Third, he quickly was seized by Jews and falsely accused of bringing Gentiles to the temple area (vv. 27–29). Fourth, he was beaten severely and was nearly killed (vv. 30–32). Fifth, he was arrested by the Roman authorities who did not really know what the fuss was all about (vv. 33–36). Sixth, he was finally allowed to speak to the Jews and give his testimony, but as soon as he told the part about taking his message to the Gentiles, the crowd erupted with shouts of "He's not fit to live!" (Acts 21:37–22:22). Seventh, because it was discovered that Paul was a Roman citizen, he was protected by the Roman authorities and allowed to address the Sanhedrin. This ended in such a dispute that the Roman commander feared Paul would be torn to pieces. So the troops put him in the barracks (Acts 22:23–23:10). Eighth, a report from Paul's nephew led the Roman authorities to transfer Paul in the middle of the night to keep him from being murdered (Acts 23:12–22). Ninth, Paul testified before King Agrippa before the scenario was over (Acts 26). Tenth, as a consequence of his testimony before the governors Festus and Felix, in which he requested that he be heard by Caesar, Paul was eventually put on a ship and sent to Rome (Acts 24–28).

There are at least three opinions regarding Paul's decision to go to Jerusalem: (1) he was led by the Spirit to go as he said; (2) he disobeyed the Holy Spirit; (3) God let the entire scenario remain an enigma so we will not be discouraged when things don't make sense for us. I will defend all three positions below.

The view that Paul was obeying the Spirit

First, let me defend the view that Paul was absolutely right to go on to Jerusalem despite warnings. We could infer this because of his apostolic authority and bold claim that he was "compelled" by the Holy Spirit to go to Jerusalem (Acts 20:22). That is weighty. Second, he got to give his testimony to many Jews in Jerusalem (Acts 22:2–22). This is something he longed to do. He also put his case before the Sanhedrin (Acts 23:1–9). This too was something he wanted to do. Third, he testified before Felix the governor, emphasizing "righteousness, self-control, and the coming judgment," producing fear in Felix (Acts 24:25). This is a tremendous witness. It gives a side of Paul's preaching we only receive from this account. Fourth, his standing before King Agrippa fulfilled a prophetic word that he would one day stand before kings (Acts 9:15; 26:1–32). Finally, after testifying to the Sanhedrin and being put in the barracks by the Romans, the Lord Jesus Himself stood by Paul and told him, "Take courage, Paul. For as you have testified about Me in Jerusalem, so you must also testify at Rome" (Acts 23:11). The Lord's word sounds like a seal on Paul's decision to go to Jerusalem.

The view that Paul disobeyed the Spirit

In examining the view that Paul disobeyed the Spirit, let us go from the general to the particular. First, very little good came from Paul's insistence that he go to Jerusalem.

One could almost make a case that nothing substantially good came of it. Second, he got into trouble almost non-stop from the moment he arrived in Jerusalem. His visit was not appreciated by anyone—whether the believing Jews he wanted to impress or the unconverted Jews he testified to. He was not in good form when standing before the Sanhedrin. He seems to have lost his temper before the high priest and, amazingly, claimed he did not know who the high priest was (Acts 23:3–5). Third, although he was called to be a minister to the Gentiles, he struggled with this. Not only was he called to be the apostle to the Gentiles, but also God gave him great success with them. Yes, this is where he succeeded—with Gentiles! His heart, however, was still in trying to convert Jews!

Paul was determined

I take the view that Paul was so determined to go to Jerusalem—and personally present the gifts to the poor people in the church there (Acts 24:17)—that he sincerely believed he was obeying the Holy Spirit. He was not consciously disobeying the Spirit. He was too wrapped up in his own desire to go to Jerusalem, no matter the cost. There is no doubt that he did not consider his life dear. "I consider my life worth nothing to me" (Acts 20:24, NIV). That is why he did not care what happened to him in Jerusalem. But his appealing to Caesar (Acts 25:12) suggests that he vindicated those prophecies about him that he should not go to Jerusalem. He might even say that they were right, but so was he.

I take the view that the prophecies to Paul in Acts 21 were from the Holy Spirit.

The enigma

Do we need to know for sure? We all have enigmas. I have many questions I want to ask about divine guidance when I get to heaven. I have had times I *know* I was in God's presence and others in which I *think* I was in His presence. The greatest freedom, as my friend Pete Cantrell says, is "having nothing to prove."

Here is the bottom line when it comes to Paul's controversy with prophecies to him: "I want you to know, brothers, that the things which have happened to me have resulted in advancing the gospel" (Phil. 1:12). That's good enough, is it not?

When Paul wrote his epistles, you can believe every word he said. He wrote the word of God. But when we see him as a person in the Book of Acts, we see him as a human being who was not perfect. And why should he be seen as perfect? If Moses, the greatest man in the Old Testament, was not perfect, why should Paul, the greatest person in the New Testament next to Jesus, have to be perfect?

CHAPTER 6

Integrity

Finally, brothers, whatever things true, whatever
things are honest, whatever things are just, whatever
things are pure, whatever things are lovely, whatever
things are of good report, if there is any virtue,
and if there is any praise, think on these things.
—Philippians 4:8

The truth shall set you free.
—John 8:32

O NE OF MY earliest memories from childhood was
when I was six years old. In my Nazarene church on
Bath Avenue in Ashland, Kentucky, a particular Sunday
evening service is etched in my memory. Looking back,
I would say it was a typical service. The people began
shouting, running, jumping up and down, walking, and
crying. My own mother ran from one side of the church
to the other in front of the altar, raising her arms in
the air with a handkerchief in one hand and shouting.
Though it was a typical service, it is the only one in which
I remember my mother carrying on like that, which is
partly why it stands out in my memory.

I found this embarrassing, even at the age of six. I
walked outside during the service. The church's janitor

found me outside and asked, "What are you doing out here, RT?"

I replied, "I don't like the noise." I had managed to slip out of the church without my parents noticing. The janitor related this to my father, who repeated the story many times.

Jesus said that we must become like a child if we want to enter the kingdom of heaven (Matt. 18:3). We could say many things about children generally and draw from these characteristics to decide what Jesus meant by this statement. But I am sure of one reason He said this: a child does not repress his expression or take care to say the right thing. A child can be guileless and transparently honest. I think that described me at the age of six when I walked out of that church service.

I am not criticizing my old church, although I would understand if you thought I was. I was brought up in my Ashland church when, I think, there was a vestige of a revival atmosphere that came from two sources: (1) the way Nazarenes were in the early twentieth century and (2) the aftermath of the Cane Ridge Revival—an area about a hundred miles from Ashland. The people in Ashland had a nickname for our church: "Noisyrenes." They were certainly right about that. Nazarenes then were noisy.

But no more; that is gone. For good or bad, those days for Nazarenes are over, and have been for years.

As you perhaps can imagine, I have thought about this aspect of my church background countless times. I have asked: What was the fuss all about? Why did they shout? Why did they run up and down the church aisles? Why did they cry? Why all the noise?

My honest answer is this: there was something very genuine—I would call it true revival—that originally brought it on. Whether it be the Cane Ridge Revival of 1801 (part of America's Second Great Awakening) or the glory days of the Church of the Nazarene (founded by Methodist leader Phineas Bresee in 1909)—neither of which were Charismatic or Pentecostal, they were known for their noise. During the Cane Ridge Revival, "the noise was like the roar of Niagara," wrote one participant.[1] Like the roar of Niagara Falls, the people could be heard a mile away. What caused the noise? People shouting. It was similar to what you hear at a football match in Britain or a baseball game in America when the home team scores. Yes, they did that in church.

But why? It was the joy of the Lord. The presence of God was so powerful that people lost their awareness of personal dignity; they did not care what people thought. They expressed their joy in their shouting and laughter and jumping up and down.

Personally I never did this. I do not know why, but I never fell into it. And yet I did not question the genuineness of some of those who did.

The purpose of this chapter is not to assess the validity of the manifestations of my old church. This chapter is about integrity—the willingness to get to the bottom of the truth no matter where it leads or what it takes to get there.

The pursuit of integrity is about the quest for truth. Or facts. It is only truth that sets one free (John 8:32). It is freedom that demonstrates the true presence of the Holy

Spirit (2 Cor. 3:17). The question is, do we really want the truth? How far are we willing to go to get to the truth?

Invoking the Oath

One thing that should surely bring about acute honesty is the consciousness that we are in God's presence. The appeal to the presence of God is like swearing an oath. If you swear an oath, you had better be sure you have authority to do so. The prophet Samuel invoked the presence of God in the declaration of his integrity. "Here I am; testify against me before the LORD and before his anointed. Whose ox have I taken? Or whose donkey have I taken? Or whom have I defrauded? Whom have I oppressed? Or from whose hand have I taken a bribe to blind my eyes with it? Testify against me and I will restore it to you" (1 Sam. 12:3, ESV). The people testified that Samuel had been transparently honest in his dealings with them.

The prophet Jeremiah had a rival. His name was Hananiah. Jeremiah prophesied that the Babylonian captivity would last seventy years. Hananiah invoked the presence of the Lord to claim the captivity would last only two years. Hananiah boldly proclaimed, "Thus says the LORD: Even so I will break the yoke of Nebuchadnezzar king of Babylon from the neck of all the nations within the space of two full years" (Jer. 28:11). Jeremiah said to Hananiah, "'Listen now, Hananiah. The LORD has not sent you, and you make this people trust in a lie. Therefore thus says the LORD: I am about to cast you from off the face of the earth. This year you shall die, because you have taught rebellion against the LORD.' So Hananiah the prophet died the same year in the seventh month" (vv. 15–17).

The point is, if one claims to be speaking for God Himself, he had better be sure he is not being deceived. It is a scary thing to say, "Thus says the Lord." It is far better we never do this than to get it wrong.

Paul invoked the presence of the Lord when he used his apostolic authority to deliver an incestuous man—a believer—to Satan. "For indeed, though absent in body but present in spirit, I have already, as if I were present, judged him who has done this deed, in the name of our Lord Jesus Christ. When you are assembled, along with my spirit, in the power of our Lord Jesus Christ, deliver him to Satan for the destruction of the flesh, so that the spirit may be saved on the day of the Lord Jesus" (1 Cor. 5:3–5).

In other words, whenever we invoke the presence of the Lord, it behooves us absolutely to be people of unquestioned integrity. We had better know what we are doing. I did it once—only once—during my twenty-five years in Westminster. It was when certain members were living in open sin and would not repent. The worst thing one could do is to invoke God's presence and not be in pursuit of the truth. It would result in judgment from the throne of God. As it turned out, the effect of Paul's invoking the presence of God as he did was that the incestuous man came to his senses and repented (2 Cor. 2:6–9). When I invoked the presence of the Lord at Westminster, the people climbed down from their arrogance and eventually came to live godly lives.

The issue is whether we are in pursuit of the truth—wherever it leads.

There are those of us who don't want to see a physician because we are afraid of what we might learn about our physical condition. So we delay going to the doctor. But surely this is wrong! Surely we should *want* to know if there is something wrong.

So too in the pursuit of integrity. We will not begin to achieve it until we do what it takes to get to the truth—about ourselves, about others, about what we teach about the Bible, about our theology, and about anything pertaining to true facts we can find. It means being even-handed, impartial, rising above ourselves, and accepting input from friends and critics in order to arrive at the objective truth. The process can be exceedingly painful. But the liberty that follows is worth the embarrassment we may experience along the way.

My previously mentioned experience as a six-year-old has, I think, made me extremely cautious over the years. I watched my Nazarene peers raise their hands in worship, shout, and outwardly show their joy in the Lord. I have made doubly sure that I don't manifest in the flesh. Some might say I have been too cautious, but I just don't want to settle for less than the real thing.

I wrote an article a few years ago for *Ministry Today* titled "Sheer Integrity."[2] It was when the so-called Lakeland Revival was in progress. I was surprised by how many people swallowed it hook, line, and sinker. Many of them were sorry later. In my opinion the whole thing was largely a fraud. Whatever were people thinking?

We live in a time when, at least in some places, there is

no theological foundation by which to judge the true and the false. People are swept up by every wind of doctrine. "My people are destroyed for lack of knowledge," said the ancient prophet (Hos. 4:6). It is the lack of knowledge of God's ways, His Word, and His wisdom that has resulted in the abundance of bubbleheads, flakes, and charlatans.

My friend Kenny Borthwick, a Scottish minister and an able Charismatic leader, says that he often watches Christian TV through the eyes and ears of a non-Christian. He said to his wife, "If I did not know better and judged Christianity by what I see on television, I would honestly think that the Christian faith is all about money."

One of the worse developments to emerge in America is the church growth movement, designed to help churches grow. Whereas in the earliest church it was the Lord who added to the church, today human manipulation, ingenuity, and motivation techniques are often used to bring about growth. Expository preaching has been largely replaced by motivational preaching. The emphasis on the miraculous has been supplanted by prosperity teaching.

Can God use these? Of course He can. My own church background was far from perfect, but God used it to save me and countless others.

"Keep the Glory Down"

I said earlier that Dr. Martyn Lloyd-Jones used to say to me, "Don't forget your Nazarene background." He explained to me why he said this. He had just read a biography of Dr. Phineas Bresee, the founder of the Church of the Nazarene. Bresee felt that the Methodists had lost the anointing that made them what they once were, so he founded the new movement. Dr. Lloyd-Jones told me that he discerned by reading Bresee's biography that there was something very genuine about the early Nazarenes. They were at the bottom of the socioeconomic class in America. They had no wealthy people and no highly educated people. They had one thing going for them: *the presence of God.* Bresee called it "the glory." In his final years Bresee had one message as he went from church to church: "Keep the glory down." The "glory," for whatever reason, was consistently characterized by people shouting, running, jumping, and crying. It was the norm for a good while. Bresee felt that if the church lost the "glory," they were finished. They became the fastest-growing denomination in America in their early years. The best of Methodism was a carryover to the Nazarenes.

As for the Cane Ridge Revival, which preceded the Nazarenes by more than a hundred years, the phenomenom was much the same—perhaps more powerful, however. It only lasted a few days, during which time hundreds were on the ground from the power of the Spirit. Nobody pushed them, and nobody prayed for them. They just fell, staying flat out on the ground for hours. They not only lost self-consciousness; some for a while lost consciousness. They were feared dead. But after a few hours, they arose to shout and cry with all their might—uninhibited— because of undoubted assurance of their salvation. The shouting phenomenon spread to denominations all over the South—mainly Methodists, Baptists, Presbyterians, and Disciples of Christ. This too is gone today. One could say that these denominations have been somewhat succeeded by the Pentecostal and Charismatic movements.

Issue: How Self-Conscious Are We?

I talked with some British missionaries a few years ago who had seen genuine revival in Africa in the mid-twentieth century. They said that one of the main characteristics of the revival was that people ceased to be conscious of how they looked. Some would beat their chests with great conviction of sin, not caring what others thought.

If these reports of the presence of God are valid, this is truly interesting. When we are in His presence, we cease to care what people think; when His presence subsides, we become all too aware of what people think. This is a pretty good rule of thumb for whether we are living in God's presence. If we are overly concerned with what people think of us—always looking over our shoulders for approval—it is likely a dead giveaway that we not in God's presence as we might be. The more we sense His presence, the less concerned we are with what people think.

Integrity and God's Presence

Two things are interconnected when it comes to integrity and God's presence. First, integrity will lead us to dwell in His presence. Second, integrity will keep us honest when it comes to assessing whether His true presence is being manifested. To put it another way: integrity leads to the presence of God; the presence of God leads to integrity. But once integrity, for any reason, begins to diminish, so too will the presence of God begin to be sensed less and less. The worst scenario is that if the presence of God is on the wane in stages and we don't recognize it, then we become like Joseph and Mary who continued on without Jesus when they thought they had Him.

There are two possibilities if we leave Jesus behind: either we find Him, or we keep on going and never come back.

I'm thinking of some high-profile preachers who once knew great power in preaching and healing. But when the anointing lifted and these ministers carried on as if the anointing had not lifted, the result was sometimes disaster. Some ended up in financial impropriety, some in sexual immorality, and some in alcoholism.

Integrity is being *governed by the truth, even when it hurts.* That's my definition.

According to the psalmist, a blameless man "keeps an oath even when it hurts" (Ps. 15:4, NIV). In ancient times the oath having been sworn was the zenith of dependability; it was the pinnacle of what one could rely on to be true. A promise might be broken, but never the oath! And yet King Saul swore an oath to his own flesh and blood—his son Jonathan—and broke it (1 Sam. 19:6–10).

Jesus told us not to swear at all. A person swears an oath to get credibility. We all want to be believed. Swearing an oath ensures that the truth is being told, that a promise will be kept. Jesus said what He did regarding the oath for two reasons. First, it was to show His understanding and application of the third command not to misuse God's name. Second, we should always tell the truth without having to back up our statements with an oath (Matt. 5:33–37). We certainly should keep our oaths even when it is painful, but we should keep *any* word we utter even when it may cost us.

The Fruit of Integrity

We should be governed by the truth, then, even when it hurts. The fruit of integrity is four things: (1) trustworthiness with money, (2) purity in morality, (3) reliability in word, and (4) hunger for the truth—or the facts.

1. Trustworthiness with money

Jesus had more to say about money than any other subject. John Wesley said that the last part of a person to be converted is his wallet! Voltaire (1694–1778) said that when it comes to money, every person's religion is the same. Or as we say in Kentucky, "When a fellow says, 'It ain't the money; it's the principle,' it's the money."

Being squeaky clean with money will keep us out of a lot of trouble. The love of money is a root of all evil (1 Tim. 6:10), so transparent honesty with money matters is required of every servant of Christ.

Integrity is not for sale. The one who has integrity cannot be bought off. Balaam was a man who gave the outward appearance of integrity. He boasted, "If Balak gave me his house full of silver and gold, I am not able to go beyond the command of the LORD my God, to do less or more" (Num. 22:18). That sounded so impressive. But it was sheer hypocrisy. Balaam did not tell Balak that God had already spoken clearly to him from the start: "You will not go with them. You will not curse the people [Israel] because they are blessed" (v. 12). Not only that; Balaam further exposed his greed for Balak's money when he said, "Now please remain here tonight, that I may know what more the LORD will say to me" (v. 19). He hoped that God would somehow change His mind! Balaam tried and tried to gain money from Balak, but God overruled (Num. 23:1–24:14). Overcome by the love of money, Balaam was a tragic figure and was eventually killed by the sword (Num. 31:7).

Balaam was for sale. The person of integrity cannot be swayed by money, but too many people can be bought if the price is right. It could even influence what they claim to believe. Upton Sinclair (1878–1968) said, "It is difficult to get a man to understand something, when his salary depends on his not understanding it."[3] I wonder how many people in churches or Christian ministry keep their jobs only as long as they champion the party line.

Maintaining integrity may mean the "road less traveled," as poet Robert Frost (1874–1963) put it:

> I shall be telling this with a sigh
> Somewhere ages and ages hence:
> Two roads diverged in a wood, and I—
> I took the one less traveled by,
> And that has made all the difference.[4]

If taking the road less traveled means getting to the truth, it is more precious than gold. "With all your getting, get understanding. Exalt her, and she will promote you; she will bring you honor, when you embrace her. She will place on your head an ornament of grace; a crown of glory she will deliver to you" (Prov. 4:7–9).

2. Purity in morality

Transparent integrity and sexual purity go together. People want their leaders to have their sexual appetites under control. The followers may or may not be so disciplined, but they certainly want their leaders to be disciplined. Fair or unfair, that is the way it is. There is a price to pay for being high profile. Those of us who are out front have a responsibility to set the example. "The price of greatness is responsibility," said Winston Churchill.[5] But we are seeing a dearth of greatness on the horizon today—at an almost inconceivable level: in the church, in politics, in government, in education, in science. I fear that irresponsible people often get to the top. Too many people in top positions have undisciplined private lives: broken marriages, secret affairs, and no strong convictions regarding being sexually pure. This refers equally to heterosexual and homosexual activity. The concept of monogamous heterosexual marriage as the biblical norm has disintegrated. More and more children are being raised in single-parent homes, and one of the consequences of this is young people growing up with confused sexual identification.

Some people who emphasize the gifts of the Holy Spirit (as in 1 Corinthians 12:8–10) don't seem to realize that these gifts have little or nothing to do with integrity—that is, one may be devoid of integrity and still see their gifts flourish. It is disappointing that this can be the case, but it should not surprise us, because gifts are "irrevocable," or as the King James puts it, "without repentance" (Rom. 11:29). This means that one's personal godliness or integrity does not come into play and thus explains how King Saul prophesied by the Spirit of God on his way to kill David (1 Sam. 19:23–24). Strange as it may seem, people with extraordinary gifts dazzle the public while their private lives make the angels blush. I have talked with people who are on the inside track regarding famous television preachers. Thankfully there are some good people on Christian TV, but it is shocking to discover how some who are sexually impure nevertheless have successful ministries.

We shall all stand before the judgment seat of Christ and give an account of the things we have done, "whether good or bad" (2 Cor. 5:10, NIV). A Methodist lay preacher who spoke while standing on a fallen tree on the first Sunday morning of the Cane Ridge Revival chose 2 Corinthians 5:10 as his text. Hundreds and hundreds fell to the ground under the power of the Holy Spirit at this service. I wish we had his sermon notes. The very fact that a text like that would be used on that unforgettable day and be so owned by God Himself shows the urgency and relevance to deal with the subject of the final judgment. Here's the point: we all must give an account of the things done while in the *body*.

First Corinthians 3:14–15 includes the promise that when a Christian's works are tested by fire and survive, that Christian will receive a reward, but if the works don't survive the fire, the Christian will still be saved but "as one escaping through the flames" (NIV). All things will be laid bare on that day (Rom. 2:16). If, for example, I receive a reward at the judgment seat of Christ, it will not be based on how well known I was on earth, how many sermons I preached, or how many books I wrote. Any reward I have will be directly related to the kind of man I am—as a father, husband, and godly person in my private, personal life. If you receive a reward, it will not be based on how much money you made, how many homes or cars you owned, or how popular you were in your church. It will come down to you as a man, as a woman. Were you faithful in marriage? Were you forgiving toward your enemy? Were you a thankful person or a complainer?

The presence of the Lord at the Cane Ridge Revival was not manifested in any of the gifts of the Holy Spirit as far as we can tell. God's presence flowed from preaching that reflected the need to be right with God in every possible way. The horror of not being right with God is what brought the terror of the Lord in many falling to the ground. No wonder they were ecstatic beyond words when they were given assurance of being saved!

3. *Reliability in word*

This means that what you say is true, and what you say you will do. You do not overclaim; that is, claim more to be true than is true. Neither do you promise to do what you know you cannot do. You can therefore be depended on to tell the truth; you can also be relied on to keep your promise.

> Lord, who will abide in Your tabernacle? Who will dwell in Your holy hill? He who walks uprightly, and does righteousness, and speaks truth in his heart; he who does not slander with the tongue and does no evil to his neighbor, nor bears a reproach against his friend; in whose eyes a vile person is

despised, but who honors those who fear the LORD;
he who swears to avoid evil and does not change.
—PSALM 15:1–4

Godliness means to be like God. It is impossible for
God to lie (Heb. 6:18; Titus 1:2). We believe God's Word
is true; we believe He can be depended on to keep His
Word. Likewise, people depend on us to keep our word
to them.

Since integrity means to be governed by the truth, even
when it hurts, this includes everyday speaking—telling
the truth, not telling lies. We all came from our mother's
womb speaking lies (Ps. 58:3). This is why a child does
not need to be trained to lie, but we all need to be trained
to tell the truth—before we are converted! But once we
come to Christ, who *is* truth (John 14:6), we are indwelled
by the "Spirit of truth" (v. 17). This means if we walk in
the Spirit, we only speak the truth—but do so in love
(Eph. 4:15)!

Simple honesty with words, transparency in conversation, reporting what is true, not speaking deceit—that is
integrity with words. But so also is keeping your word
when you make a promise, fulfilling your commitment,
being there when you say you will be there, paying up
what you said you would pay. This is integrity with words.

On the other hand, the devil is a liar, a murderer from
the beginning, and the father of lies. When he lies, he
speaks his "native language" (John 8:44, NIV). Satan has
no integrity—not even a trace. As Satan is the opposite of God, good, godly, true, lovely, and praiseworthy,
you and I should seek to emulate the opposite of the

devil, who is bad, ugly, hateful, hurtful, defeating, and counterproductive.

4. Hunger for the truth—or the facts

How much do we want the truth? Are we willing to do what it takes to find what is true? What if it means having to abandon certain cherished positions that may or may not be true? Are we willing for our position to be challenged?

I had a hard decision to make some years ago when I came to a different position on Hebrews 6:4–6. I had not only preached but had put in writing that these verses refer to people not truly saved—the classic Reformed position. In the summer of 1982 I came to see that these verses clearly refer to saved people who had become stone deaf to the Holy Spirit and consequently could not be renewed again to repentance. I had a decision to make: Should I go public with my view that they are saved people? Yes, but it was a hard decision. And yet I did so immediately. The renewal of anointing was more important than pleasing those with the Reformed view.

I know people who would not be willing to change their position only because they have already taken a stand in writing. They fear their reputation too much to admit they might have been wrong in the past. This is not humility at work, and I fear that such people will probably never be able to grow theologically once they dig in their heels like that.

Walking in the Spirit not only means we will tell the truth; walking in the Spirit also means walking in the light. Walking in the light means walking into what may be undiscovered truth for us. It is not easy to climb down from a view for which we have become known, but the question is, what is more important to us—an increased anointing, which is on offer if we walk in the light, or staying where we are to save face?

But there is more—something very important. We must come to the truth but equally come into graciousness. Graciousness means overlooking faults. Graciousness is total forgiveness. Graciousness is keeping no record of wrongs (1 Cor. 13:5, NIV). Jesus was full of grace and truth (John 1:17). Some are full of truth but not full of grace. Some are full of grace but short on truth. Is this possible? Yes. This should caution us that we should aspire to graciousness as much as we do the truth. The consequence will be meekness—a rare jewel. If we are meek, we will welcome criticism. We won't retort or become offensively defensive.

The expression "real deal" comes to mind. People will ask me of a certain person: "Is he (or she) the real deal?" People want to believe that their heroes are genuine. Real. That they won't become the center of a scandal at some point down the road.

Let us do all in our strength to be the real deal by living with transparent integrity.

The essence of integrity is an unfeigned love of the truth—whatever it is or wherever it leads—but truth with graciousness. The proof of integrity is that we will do what it takes, go where we must, and pay whatever the cost in order to arrive at the truth that sets us free.

That is where the presence of God is found—where truth is.

I have long been gripped by Paul's words that those who would believe a lie and consequently perish are traceable to not receiving "the love of the truth" in order to be saved (2 Thess. 2:10–12, KJV). The issue is, do we receive the love of the truth? In other words, do we love *the truth*, whatever that truth may be? Jesus said that if any of us does the Father's will, we will come to the truth (John 7:17). That is the bottom line: Is the truth what we want?

People with integrity want the truth more than anything in the world.

Whatever happened to integrity?

Caution About Integrity

The danger of integrity is that one can become self-righteous about it. Integrity alone gives no guarantee of a happy ending or finishing well. Self-righteousness is always nearby to squeeze its way in. Self-righteousness is the hardest thing to see in ourselves but so easy to see in others.

You and I must strive to maintain integrity without taking ourselves so seriously. Self-righteousness and integrity don't mix well; self-righteousness coming alongside integrity is like a dead fly giving perfume "a bad smell," much in the way that "a little folly outweighs wisdom and honor" (Eccles. 10:1, NIV). Never forget that the person with the highest level of integrity still has a heart that is vile, deceitful, and capable of being obnoxious. Let us allow this for our heroes.

Job is a good example. He was blameless, as perfect as one could be—for a while! But when the pressure was on,

Job's self-righteousness began to seep through the cracks until he became unbearable to be around. He said to those who were taunting him: "I will never admit you are in the right; till I die, *I will not deny my integrity.* I will maintain my innocence and never let go of it; my conscience will not reproach me as long as I live" (Job 27:5–6, NIV, emphasis added).

This is so sad, but fortunately God had mercy on him and he came to his senses. Never forget that self-righteousness is as vile in God's sight as any sin you can think of is in our sight!

Maintaining integrity requires that we are always seeking the truth and graciousness. We need to be open to how self-righteous and *set in our ways* we are as we seek what is true. That should keep us humble. If we want to get to the bottom of things, we must see our sinfulness while being open to the truth that may surprise us. We do this, if possible, to get to the facts. It is not enough that we did it yesterday; we must do it today.

The reward for integrity is the manifest presence of God. The reward for dwelling in His presence is integrity. That's a pretty good deal if you ask me.

CHAPTER 7

Symbols of God's Presence

When you see the ark of the covenant of the LORD
your God and the Levite priests carrying it, then
you shall set out from where you are and go behind
it. There must be a distance of two thousand cubits
between you and it. Do not draw closer to it, in
order that you may know the way you should
go. For you have not passed this way before.
—JOSHUA 3:3–4

They [the priests] serve in a sanctuary that
is an example and shadow of the heavenly
one, as Moses was instructed by God when
he was about to make the tabernacle, "See
that you make all things according to the
pattern shown you on the mountain."
—HEBREWS 8:5

DURING THE ERA of the Mosaic law (c. 1300 BC
to AD 33), God gave Moses basically two things:
teaching and miracles. You could say these anticipated
what we call the Word and the Spirit. The Word included
the moral law (the Ten Commandments), the ceremo-
nial law (how the people of Israel should worship God),
and the civil law (how the people of God should govern

themselves). The Spirit was seen in things such as the lightning at Sinai, the thick cloud over the mountain, the daily manna, and supernatural guidance by the pillar of cloud and fire. The Word was not only for the teaching of God's ancient people but also for us today. "For whatever was previously written was written for our instruction, so that through perseverance and encouragement of the Scriptures we might have hope" (Rom. 15:4).

Mixing the Presence and Symbols of the Presence

During this period there was a surprising mixture between the symbols and God's actual presence. The symbols pointed to the coming of Christ and the Holy Spirit—over thirteen hundred years later—and the real presence of the Lord. Such symbols included the tabernacle generally and things in the tabernacle particularly—the bread, the incense, the lampstand, the most holy place, and the ark of the covenant.

> In the first part of the tabernacle, called the Holy Place, were the candlestick, the table, and the showbread. Behind the second veil was the second part of the tabernacle called the Most Holy Place, which contained the golden censer and the ark of the covenant overlaid with gold, containing the golden pot holding the manna, Aaron's rod that budded, and the of the covenant. Above the ark were the cherubim of glory overshadowing the mercy seat.
> —HEBREWS 9:2–5

Even though Moses gave them these symbols, God had a way of revealing Himself immediately and directly from time to time. In other words, these symbols pointed to the future coming of Christ and the Holy Spirit, *but* there came also an extraordinary display of the manifest presence of God in Moses's day and at various times later on. So whereas things such as the tabernacle and the ark of the covenant were symbolic for the future fulfillment, God had a way of manifesting Himself during this period in an astonishing manner.

During the forty-year period in the wilderness the immediate and direct presence of the Lord was, as I said, manifested by the cloud by day and the fire by night. These supernatural manifestations of God's presence were given to the children of Israel primarily for guidance.

> When the cloud was lifted up from over the tabernacle, the children of Israel would set out in all their journeys. But if the cloud was not lifted up, then they did not set out until the day that it was lifted. For the cloud of the LORD was on the tabernacle by day, and fire was on it by night, in the sight of all the house of Israel, throughout all their journeys.
>
> —EXODUS 40:36–38

I often think we have an interesting occurrence in our day—of symbols only! Whether it be the burning of incense in the more liturgical churches or the manufactured smoke in the services of some Charismatic churches, there is a curious absence of the real presence of God! Some churches have pictures of doves. Some churches have the waving of flags, which look like fire from a distance. But so often the symbols are all there is—just the symbols.

Many believers long for the true presence of God to emerge in churches where there so often seem to be symbols only. I suspect that with the diminishing of the genuine presence of God, there is an increase of symbols.

Symbols: The Tabernacle

The tabernacle—a tent—in the wilderness was erected under Moses's leadership. And yet Moses merely built it according to a divine plan. Creative though Moses may have been, he was not given liberty to do as he thought best; he had to follow instructions. Everything pertaining to the tabernacle—the ark, the table, the lampstand, had to be carried out "according to their pattern which was shown to you on the mountain" (Exod. 25:40). After all, what Moses made was a "shadow" of what was in heaven (Heb. 8:5).

In other words, the *real*—or the original—is in heaven. All that was on earth was a copy of the real. What is more, the tabernacle pointed forward to two fulfillments: the coming of the Lord Jesus Christ and of the Holy Spirit. All that is in the tabernacle pointed to these. Since this book focuses on the presence of God, let us see how the tabernacle pointed to this.

First, there were the two compartments of the tabernacle: the holy place and the most holy place—also called the holy of holies. This was at times referred to as the tent of meeting. It was where God met with Moses and spoke to him face-to-face (Exod. 33:7-11).

The holy place

In the first room—the holy place—there were the table, the lampstand, and the altar of incense. On the table was the bread, called showbread or bread of the presence. The bread was eaten by the priests and was once used in an emergency for David when he was on the run (1 Sam. 21:6). The bread pointed to Jesus—who called Himself the "bread of life" (John 6:48). The bread also pointed to the Lord's Supper—bread being the symbolic body of Jesus. "I tell you the truth, unless you eat the flesh of the Son of Man and drink His blood, you have no life in you" (v. 53).

Indeed, the Lord's Supper—the Eucharist, or Holy Communion—was God's symbolic presence. Roman Catholics teach that the bread and wine are literally the body and blood of Jesus once the priest proclaims "This is my body...this my blood." This is called transubstantiation. Martin Luther came up with a view he called consubstantiation—that the bread and wine are paired with His body and blood. Ulrich Zwingli regarded the Lord's Supper as only a *memorial* of Jesus's death on the cross. John Calvin believed that Jesus is *spiritually* present in the Lord's Supper when we believe this by faith. Indeed, when we by faith partake of the bread and wine as Christ being spiritually present, there can be a great sense of His presence in a manner promised uniquely in the Lord's Supper.

Perhaps not so well known is the fact that the prelude to the Cane Ridge Revival was at a small church on the Red River in Kentucky, just north of the Tennessee-Kentucky border. The power of God was manifested at the Lord's

Supper in a manner that led directly to the Cane Ridge Revival.

The Lord's Supper is so sacred that God sent judgment on certain Christians at Corinth. Because they partook in a manner "unworthily"—that was, showing contempt for certain members of the church, God sent illness and sometimes death to these believers (1 Cor. 11:21–32).

Also in the first room of the tabernacle was the altar of incense. This was to be burning continually. It was positioned next to the curtain that separated the holy place from the most holy place. The aroma went through the curtain, making its way into the holy of holies, symbolizing the prayers of God's people. Prayer is to be made continually before God, for our prayers are a sweet smell to God that wafts into His very presence. In the Book of Revelation we are told that an angel "was given much incense to offer with the prayers of all the saints on the golden altar before the throne. The smoke of the incense, with the prayers of the saints, ascended before God from the angel's hand" (Rev. 8:3–4). This is a reminder that all our prayers are special to God, that they are bottled up in heaven—only to be poured out in His time.

The golden lampstand, the menorah with its seven branches, is what gave illumination in the holy place. Otherwise the priests would not be able to walk around in the tabernacle at night. Jesus fulfilled this when He said, "I am the light of the world. Whoever follows Me shall not walk in darkness, but shall have the light of life" (John 8:12).

The most holy place

The second room is the most holy place. This represented the immediate presence of God. A curtain separated the holy place from the most holy place, or holy of holies. In the most holy place was the ark of the covenant. This was the most sacred and fearful item of all. Inside the ark were the tablets of stone on which God wrote the Ten Commandments, a jar of manna, and Aaron's rod that budded (Heb. 9:3–4). On top of the ark was a slab of gold—called the mercy seat. Only one man—the high priest—could enter the most holy place. And this was done only once a year—on the Day of Atonement. A bell was tied to his ankle so it could be heard outside. A rope was also tied to his ankle so that he could be dragged out in the event he should die or be struck dead. The high priest never entered the most holy place without the blood of an animal. He would sprinkle the blood on the mercy seat.

When we remember that the tabernacle was a copy of the true tabernacle in heaven, it is a reminder that there is a heavenly mercy seat. Jesus entered heaven "by His own blood" (Heb. 9:12) and sprinkled it on the heavenly mercy seat. It was at the mercy seat that the atonement of Christ took effect.

When Moses finished the work, God put His seal on the tabernacle. "Then the cloud covered the tent of meeting, and the glory of the LORD filled the tabernacle. Moses was not able to enter the tent of meeting because the cloud had settled on it, and the glory of the LORD filled the tabernacle" (Exod. 40:34–35).

This is what I mean regarding the *real* presence of God mixing with the symbol. The tabernacle was a symbol; all the things in the tabernacle were symbols, and yet God manifested His visible presence in the original tabernacle. He would do this later at the dedication of Solomon's temple. When the ark was brought into the temple, "the cloud filled the house of the LORD, so that the priests could not continue to minister because of the cloud, for the glory of the LORD filled the house of the LORD" (1 Kings 8:10–11).

The ark therefore was the most hallowed of all of the symbols. And yet the Israelites would need instructions concerning the ark that would teach them reverence. On the day the children of Israel prepared to cross over the Jordan into the Promised Land, Joshua gave instructions. They were told to keep a distance from the ark "of two thousand cubits....Do not draw closer to it" (Josh. 3:4). For the ark not only symbolized the presence of God; it also represented the awesomeness and glory of God. Here again, what was a symbol of God's presence was nonetheless very real: "When the carriers of the ark came to the Jordan, the feet of the priests carrying the ark dipped into the edge of the water....Then the water that flows down from upstream stood still and rose up in a heap very far away" (vv. 15–16). The priests who carried the ark stood firm on dry ground in the middle of the Jordan. This was reminiscent of the Israelites crossing the Red Sea on dry land. All Israel passed by the ark until the whole nation had completed the crossing on dry land (v. 17).

These things said, God would not allow the ark to be "used"—manipulated. The Israelites made a huge mistake one day. They used the ark as a superstitious symbol, as if its presence would substitute for people's responsibility.

When they lost four thousand soldiers in battle with the Philistines, they concluded that the ark's presence would have saved them. "'Let us bring the ark of the covenant of the LORD out of Shiloh to us, that it might come among us and rescue us out of the hand of our enemies.' So the people sent to Shiloh, that they might bring from there the ark of the covenant of the LORD of Hosts, who dwells above the cherubim" (1 Sam. 4:3–4). This gave the Israelites a premature sense of victory. When the "ark of the covenant of the LORD came into the camp, all Israel shouted with a great shout, so that the ground was in an uproar" (v. 5). It also produced a demoralizing of the Philistines, but that was temporary. For the Philistines fought and Israel lost thirty thousand soldiers. Not only that: the ark of God was captured (vv. 10–11).

The Israelites could not figure this out. How could this happen to them? If the ark didn't fight for them, what hope did they have? But while the ark was with the Philistines, the result was disastrous for them. Their god Dagon fell on his face before the ark. Not only that, but also "the hand of God was very heavy" on the Philistines wherever the ark went (1 Sam. 5:3, 11). The eventual consequence was that the Philistines gladly sent the ark back to Israel. But when the ark came to Beth Shemesh, some seventy of the men were suddenly put to death "because they had looked into the ark of the LORD" (1 Sam. 6:19). Whereas the ark was a symbol of God's presence, God overruled in a manner that it was more than just a symbol. When King David ordered the ark to be brought to Jerusalem, "Uzzah reached out and took hold of the ark of God because the oxen had stumbled"; immediately God struck him down, and "he died there beside the ark of God" (2 Sam. 6:6–7).

Therefore, though the Law and those things that came with the Law, such as the ark, were only shadows and not the realities themselves, God Himself was never far away. But when Jesus died on the cross, He fulfilled all the things that the Mosaic law had introduced. The Book of Hebrews shows how Jesus's death was a fulfillment of the Day of Atonement. When Jesus cried out, "It is finished" (John 19:30), He meant that the Law was fulfilled in our behalf.

God's Manifest Presence

Possibly the most extraordinary sense of God's presence of all time was on Good Friday. While Jesus was crying out, "My God, my God, why have You forsaken me?," darkness covered the land. It lasted for some three hours (Matt. 27:45–46). What was the darkness? It was the manifest presence of God. It was His glory. When Moses introduced the Day of Atonement, God said, "Speak to Aaron your brother so that he does not come at any time into the Holy Place within the veil before the mercy seat, which is on the ark, so that he will not die, for *I will appear in the cloud on the mercy seat*" (Lev. 16:2, emphasis added). Note carefully: *God Himself* would appear in the cloud. Recall that when the ark was brought into the temple, the cloud filled it. The priests could not perform their service, for the glory of the Lord filled the temple. But Solomon then said, "The Lord has said that he would dwell in thick darkness" (1 Kings 8:12). A dark cloud. That is what took place on Good Friday. It was the divine affirmation of the cross. It was God's seal on His Son's death. Darkness, the manifest presence of God, filled the earth.

But there is more. The Feast of Pentecost—meaning fifty days—came annually to commemorate the giving of the Law. The Holy Spirit came down on the disciples fifty days following the death of Jesus. As Jesus's death signified the fulfilling of the Mosaic law, so the coming of the Spirit ratified Jesus's fulfillment of it. "If you are led by the Spirit, you are not under the law" (Gal. 5:18).

The Holy Spirit would produce the awe toward the things of God that were taught by Moses and Joshua. The aftermath of Pentecost was summed up: "Everyone was filled with awe" (Acts 2:43, niv). When Ananias and Sapphira lied to the Holy Spirit and were struck dead—much like those who abused the ark—"great fear came on the entire church" (Acts 5:11). They were scared. Everybody was.

I doubt the early church needed pictures of doves to remind them of the Holy Spirit. There was no need to burn incense. Symbols are not needed when God Himself is manifestly present.

CHAPTER 8

Manifold Manifestations of God's Presence

Then they heard the sound of the LORD
God walking in the garden in the cool
of the day, and the man and his wife hid
themselves from the presence of the LORD
God among the trees of the garden.
—GENESIS 3:8

Do not be grieved, for the joy of
the LORD is your strength.
—NEHEMIAH 8:10

JONATHAN EDWARDS BELIEVED that every generation has a responsibility to discover where the sovereign Redeemer is moving, then to move in that direction.
Likewise, the task of every child of God is to discover
in which direction the Holy Spirit is moving in our lives,
and then to embrace the manner in which He chooses to
unveil His presence and direction. As God may or may
not repeat the precise manner in which His glory was
revealed to the church in a previous generation, so too
God may be pleased to show up in our lives in a way of
which you and I have not remotely thought. Eye has not

seen nor ear heard the things God has prepared for those who love Him, who wait for Him (Isa. 64:4; 1 Cor. 2:9).

The man I was named after, Dr. R. T. Williams, would say to preachers, "Honor the blood; honor the Holy Ghost." That meant to honor the blood of Jesus—extolling its power—and recognize the presence of the Holy Spirit.

Not every manifestation of God's presence is exactly the same. Not every manifestation of His presence is the "same old, same old." You may say: But did not God say, "I am the Lord, I do not change"? (Mal. 3:6). And doesn't Scripture say that "Jesus Christ is the same yesterday, and today, and forever"? (Heb. 13:8). Absolutely.

But God loves to show up in unpredictable ways. He is the same God but manifests in multitudinous ways. There are reasons for this. One reason is it challenges our faith when He shows up in a way He has not manifested Himself before. If all manifestations were the same, no faith would be required to accept His ways. We would take Him for granted, whether He manifested as the unprecedented fourth man turning up in the burning fiery furnace (Dan. 3:25) or through an angel shutting the mouths of lions (Dan. 6:22). According to Hebrews 11, some people by faith "escaped the edge of the sword" (v. 34) while others "were sawn in two…were slain with the sword" (v. 37). The opposites were accomplished *by faith*. If God did the same thing every time He chose to manifest Himself, we would have no need for faith. Some might even get tired of the supernatural. This is what happened with the children of Israel in the desert. The manna was supernatural food, and the people got tired of it (Num. 21:5). Think of that—getting tired of the supernatural! Do not think it could not happen to you and me.

I have preached many times in Wales and have never had a boring service there. I love to preach in Wales, yet I sometimes get the feeling that there are those in that country who fancy they would be the first to recognize God's next move; they think it would be the way He showed up in the great Welsh Revival of 1904–1905. During this time there was little preaching and much singing and many conversions! Furthermore, there were staunch evangelicals who objected to the Welsh Revival because they said it was unbiblical. Nevertheless, an estimated 150,000 people were saved. During the height of the revival even the pubs closed down, and the jails were largely empty. I used to enjoy hearing Mrs. Martyn Lloyd-Jones describe what it was like. She was six years old and living in London, but her father put her on a train in Paddington, London, sending her to Wales to see the move of God, even taking her out of school! When criticized for doing this, her father replied, "She can always go to school, but she may never see revival again." The Welsh Revival was an undoubted manifestation of God's presence. But God may or may not manifest that way again.

Indeed, God may show up in the future in an unprecedented manner. And yet all manifestations of the true presence of the Lord will cohere with Scripture even if there is no exact similarity in Scripture.

It is impossible to know what the presence of God was like—or what fellowship with Him was like—before the Fall in the Garden of Eden. Adam and Eve had unbroken fellowship with God before the Fall. For how long? Who knows? But they experienced the presence of the Lord God in the garden in a way you and I could not experience today.

The difference between experiencing the presence of God before the Fall and experiencing His presence in heaven is this: before the Fall humans were able to sin, but after we are glorified, believers will be unable to sin. You may recall Augustine's four stages of humankind: (1) before the Fall they were created "able to sin"; (2) after the Fall they were "unable not to sin"; (3) after conversion they are "able not to sin"; (4) after glorification they will be "unable to sin."

So what is the difference between the way Adam and Eve experienced the presence of God and the way you and I may experience Him? That is what this chapter is about.

Consciousness of Sin

Adam and Eve heard the "sound" of the Lord God (Gen. 3:8). I wonder what that was! Was it His voice? Probably. They literally heard the Lord God "walking in the garden in the cool of the day" (v. 8). That description is so interesting. What was the "cool of the day" like? It sounds so perfect. But the sound would have made them ashamed now that they had not kept faith with their Creator. God called out, "Where are you?" (v. 9). It was as though God did not find them where they normally were. What was the "sound" of His voice? Had it changed? Did His voice sound angry? Or did His voice sound sad? We only know that Adam and Eve hid themselves among the trees of the garden (v. 8). They were very ashamed.

One thing we do know about the effect of God's presence on Adam and Eve: when they sinned, they were ashamed. They were naked before the Fall with no sense of shame or embarrassment, but when they sinned, they felt the need to hide themselves from the presence of the Lord God among the trees of the garden. Their reaction shows the connection between the Lord's presence and holiness. God's presence will have an effect on our lives. According to Jesus, the first thing the Holy Spirit does when He comes to the world is to convince of sin because people do not believe (John 16:7–9). People by nature will never—ever—see their sin. Only the Holy Spirit can make people conscious of sin.

Isaiah found this out too. When he was given a glimpse of the glory of the Lord, the result was a profound conviction of sin. "Woe is me! For I am undone because I am a man of unclean lips" (Isa. 6:5). When Peter saw how Jesus caused so many fish to be caught, he fell at Jesus's knees and said, "Depart from me, for I am a sinful man, O Lord" (Luke 5:8).

A lesson from church history is this: the greatest saints always saw themselves as the greatest sinners. Tragically, one of the most ominous omissions in the church today is a sense of sin. When King Josiah read the Book of the Law, he "tore his clothes" and said, "Great is the wrath of the LORD that is kindled against us, because our fathers have not obeyed the words of this book by doing according to all that is written concerning us" (2 Kings 22:11–13).

You cannot work up this kind of remorse; the Lord's presence does it.

Joy

And yet as I said, God may be pleased to manifest Himself in a different manner from before. The same David who said, "Wash me thoroughly from my iniquity, and cleanse me from my sin" and "My sin is ever before me" (Ps. 51:2–3) also said, "In Your presence is fullness of joy" (Ps. 16:11).

In Nehemiah's day when the people "wept when they heard the words of the Law," Nehemiah stepped in to say: "Go your way. Eat the fat, drink the sweet drink...this day is holy to our Lord. Do not be grieved, for the joy of the LORD is your strength" (Neh. 8:9–10). Then the Levites calmed all the people, saying, "Hush! Because today is holy you should stop being so sorrowful" (v. 11).

God does not want us continually to beat ourselves black and blue because of our sin. He is very displeased when we do not acknowledge our sin (1 John 1:8), and He tells us that we must "not sin" (1 John 2:1). But no sooner does He say that than He adds, "If anybody does sin, we have an Advocate with the Father—Jesus Christ the Righteous One. He is the atoning sacrifice for our sins" (vv. 1–2).

Is it possible to have conviction of sin and a great sense of joy simultaneously? Yes. The sin is cleansed by our walking in the light (1 John 1:7). The result: joy. The conviction of sin may precede the joy, yes, but the sense of sin continues alongside the blissful knowledge that God has accepted us for the sake of His Son. We do not outgrow the sense of sin simply because the joy of the Lord comes in. The two apparently opposing states are the norm of the Christian life. The joy therefore becomes incalculable.

Job could say, "I despise myself and repent in dust and ashes," while at the same time being overwhelmed with the knowledge, "No purpose of yours [God's] can be thwarted" (Job 42:2, 6, NIV). Or as John Newton put it in his poem, "In Evil Long I Took Delight," "With pleasing grief and mournful joy, my spirit now is filled; that I should such a life destroy, yet live by Him I killed."

How can one have pleasing grief or mournful joy? Listen to Isaiah:

> I will not contend forever, nor will I always be angry; for the spirit would grow faint before Me, and the souls whom I have made. For the iniquity of his unjust gain I was angry and struck him; I hid My face and was wrathful, and he went on turning away in the way of his heart. I have seen his ways but will heal him; I will lead him and restore comfort to him and to his mourners, by creating the fruit of the lips.
>
> —ISAIAH 57:16–19

Also read a psalm David wrote: "For His anger endures but a moment, in His favor is life; weeping may endure for a night, but joy comes in the morning" (Ps. 30:5).

God gets our attention by convicting us of our sin, but He does not leave us in that state without coming to our rescue. So having said, "My sin is ever before me," David did not hesitate to add: "Purify me with hyssop, and I will be clean; wash me, and I will be whiter than snow. Make me to hear joy and gladness, that the bones that You have broken may rejoice" (Ps. 51:3, 7–8). Continual conviction of sin is paralleled with the joy of the Lord.

What is the joy of the Lord? It is two things: (1) the Lord's own joy—what He feels, and (2) the joy we get from seeing His joy over us! It is like John 5:44: we get our joy from knowing we have sought God's praise, not the praise of people, *and* knowing how much this pleases Him. Likewise, the Spirit of the Lord was on Jesus to "comfort all who mourn, to preserve those who mourn in Zion, to give to them beauty for ashes, the oil of joy for mourning, the garment of praise for the spirit of heaviness" (Isa. 61:2–3; see Luke 4:18).

The second fruit of the Spirit that Paul lists is joy: "The fruit of the Spirit is love, joy…" (Gal. 5:22). The disciples were "filled with joy and with the Holy Spirit" (Acts 13:52). "The kingdom of God does not mean eating and drinking, but righteousness and peace and joy in the Holy Spirit" (Rom. 14:17). "Though you do not see Him now, you believe and you rejoice with joy unspeakable and full of glory" (1 Pet. 1:8).

Fear

Strange as it may seem, one of the main manifestations of the presence of God is fear, the fear of the Lord. Whereas "the fear of man brings a snare" (Prov. 29:25), the fear of the Lord is the beginning of knowledge, wisdom, and understanding (Prov. 1:7; 9:10). And yet this kind of fear is a choice on our part. Those who did not "*choose* the fear of the LORD" were those who inherited calamity and disaster (Prov. 1:26–29).

But there have been times when the fear of the Lord was not a choice on the part of the people but God's sovereign choice of manifesting His presence. The Greek word for fear is *phobos*—from which we get our word *phobia*. *Phobos* may be translated "fear" or, more so nowadays, "awe," "amazement," or "astonishment." When Zechariah, who had been mute owing to his unbelief (Luke 1:20), suddenly spoke, the people were "filled with awe" (v. 65, NIV). When Jesus healed a man and then forgave his sins, "they were all amazed, and they glorified God and were filled with fear, saying, 'We have seen wonderful things today'" (Luke 5:26). When Jesus finished his Sermon on the Mount, the people were "astonished" at His teaching because of His authority (Matt. 7:28). I am intrigued that Jesus could produce a sense of amazement and awe from His teaching as easily as when He performed a miracle.

If mourning for sin and inexpressible joy seem contradictory, here is yet another paradox: fear and joy at the same time. That is what the disciples experienced on the morning of Jesus's resurrection. The women left the tomb "with fear and great joy" (Matt. 28:8). How can one be filled with joy and fear simultaneously? Answer: if it is the fear of the Lord's presence rather than fleshly fear, it is possible. There is a fear to be disdained. Paul said to Timothy that God has not given us a spirit of fear (which can also be translated as timidity or cowardice), but of power and love and self-control (2 Tim. 1:7).

The fear of the Lord is vastly different from human fear or anxiety. The fear of the Lord is both joyful and scary—scary because we sense how *real* God is and know that the Bible is true. There is a heaven. There is a hell. God is a

God of justice and wrath. Nothing gets scarier than that. And yet at the same time we find these realities emancipating and thrilling because the fear of God carries peace and understanding with it. During Jesus's earthly ministry this truth emerged often. "Fear came on everyone. And they glorified God, saying, 'A great prophet has risen up among us!' and 'God has visited His people!'" (Luke 7:16).

Part of the fallout from the Day of Pentecost was that "fear came to every soul" (Acts 2:43). When Ananias and Sapphira were struck dead on the spot for lying to the Holy Spirit, "great fear came on all those who heard these things" (Acts 5:5). Indeed, "great fear came on the entire church and on all those who heard these things" (v. 11).

I doubt not that this is what characterized the congregation in Enfield, Connecticut, on July 8, 1741, when Jonathan Edwards preached his sermon "Sinners in the Hands of an Angry God." As Edwards explained the coming eternal punishment and said that it was by the "mercy of God" that the people were not in hell right then, they began to hold on to church pews to keep from sliding into hell. Strong men were seen holding on to tree trunks to keep from sliding into hell.

Healing

One manifestation of God's presence may be called a healing presence. I learned this from minister Paul Cain. He would say to me, "There is such a thing as a healing presence." I had never heard a manifestation of God's presence described that way before, although it can be found in Scripture. Luke 5:17 says, "On a certain day, as

He [Jesus] was teaching, Pharisees and teachers of the law were sitting nearby, who had come from every town of Galilee and Judea and from Jerusalem. And the power of the Lord was present to heal the sick." Such a presence is sovereignly given. Humans cannot make it happen. My friend Paul experienced God's presence this way a long time ago—in the years 1951–1953, when he was in his early twenties. He said that the healing anointing lifted after those years, but that many of those involved in praying for the sick would not admit that the anointing had lifted and kept on claiming that people were being healed when more often than not they were making it up. But when the "healing presence" would come, Paul said, "virtually every sick person was healed. All the people could almost drink it in." People getting out of wheelchairs wasn't unusual, and many with polio were healed (that was before the Salk vaccine came along). Healing from nearly everything from cancer to goiters was common.

God is sovereign. He said to Moses, "I will have mercy on whom I will have mercy, and I will have compassion on whom I will have compassion" (Rom. 9:15; see Exod. 33:19). God decides. He decides who will be the next person to be saved (John 3:8). He decides who will be healed. The prayer of faith heals the sick (James 5:15). The prayer of faith is present or it isn't. We can't work it up; we can't make things like that happen. God gives the faith; faith is the gift of God. We may or may not appreciate this aspect of God's sovereignty, but this fact of the character of God needs to be recovered in our day. It is a far cry from the thinking of those who presume they can demand God to do things or that they are entitled to things. One of the curses of our age is a feeling of entitlement. It is in the world, and it is in the church. The belief in the sovereignty of God has virtually perished from certain places in the church. We need instead to go to God on bended knee for "mercy" (Heb. 4:16). The man with leprosy understood the sovereignty of God. He said to Jesus, "Lord, *if You are willing*, You can make me clean" (Matt. 8:2). A healing presence set in. "*I will*," said Jesus. "Be clean!" (v. 3, emphasis added). Immediately the man was cured.

Jesus could remotely authorize a healing presence. When He promised a Roman centurion, "I will come and heal him," referring to the centurion's servant, the centurion replied, "Lord, I am not worthy that You should come under my roof. But speak the word only, and my servant will be healed" (Matt. 8:7–8). He revealed his faith in Jesus's sovereign power by saying that Jesus did not need to go to the sick person's side—that Jesus could do it from where He was. Praising the centurion's faith, Jesus said to him, "Go your way. And as you have believed, so let it be done for you" (v. 13). The servant was healed at that very hour.

All of the people healed, cured, delivered, or helped in any way by Jesus in the four Gospels—or disciples in the Book of Acts—can be explained by the sovereign healing presence of the Holy Spirit.

Prayer

Some disciples of John the Baptist asked Jesus, "Why do we and the Pharisees fast often, but Your disciples do not fast?" He replied: "Can the guests of the bridegroom mourn as long as the bridegroom is with them? But the days will come when the bridegroom will be taken from them, and then they will fast" (Matt. 9:14–15). In saying this, Jesus was prophesying that He would be going back to heaven from whence He came. Indeed, this prophecy was fulfilled when Jesus ascended into heaven.

The first thing Jesus's disciples did after He ascended was to meet in an upper room. As I said earlier, we don't know for sure that they fasted. But one thing is for certain: they prayed. Their waiting period turned out to be a ten-day prayer meeting. "These all continued with one accord in prayer" (Acts 1:14). You may have thought that after the Holy Spirit fell on the 120 disciples, they would not need to pray anymore, but that would be wrong. Prayer became more special than ever now that the Bridegroom had been taken from them. The first description of the earliest church after Pentecost showed them doing four things: teaching, fellowshipping, breaking bread (the Lord's Supper), and praying (Acts 2:42).

A welcome manifestation of the Spirit of the Lord is a consensus, or agreement, of God's people to pray. You could call it a prayer presence, a time when people want to do nothing but pray. Have you ever felt like that?

I will describe two kinds of prayer presence. First, when it is planned. The early church had a specific time when they prayed. Peter and John were on their way to the Temple Mount because at "the ninth hour" there was a set "hour of prayer" (Acts 3:1). This scheduled prayer time was no doubt set by the apostles. Second, when it is unplanned and spontaneous. As soon as the disciples were released from the Sanhedrin—having been warned not to speak or teach in Jesus's name, "they lifted their voices in unity to God and prayed" (Acts 4:24). This kind of praying broke out again when it appeared that King Herod was going to put Peter to death. He was kept in prison, "but the church prayed to God without ceasing for him" (Acts 12:5). There is nothing like an emergency to precipitate a prayer presence.

Either kind of praying—planned or unplanned—is effectual. Prayer honors God; God honors prayer. Planned prayer would include one's daily quiet time. I have a caution for you: if you don't *plan* to give God a certain amount of time each day, you will probably never get around to it. Spontaneous prayer comes when, suddenly—possibly at the last minute—you feel the need to put everything aside and pray.

Prayer is vitally important to the person in full-time ministry. The need for deacons in the early church came about so that the apostles could give themselves "to prayer and to the ministry of the word" (Acts 6:4). Note the order: they spent time in prayer first, then ministry of the Word. It is not good when people in the ministry rush to teaching or preaching before they have spent adequate time alone with God. For too many of us, prayer gets our attention last. It should come first. One day Peter went up on a roof to pray (Acts 10:9). Little did he know that he would have a vision that would lead to the gospel being taken to Gentiles.

The wonderful thing about taking time to pray is that you never know what might happen. Whether a set time or a spontaneous moment, take advantage of any time to pray. The slightest impulse to pray is a prayer presence. Grab it. Go for it. Often when people say, "Please pray for me," I say, "Let's pray now"—and do so. Praying is never wasted time.

Following a service in my old church in Ashland one Thursday evening in April 1956, three men said to Billy Ball, a staff member at the church, "We don't want to go home; we feel like staying here to pray." He replied, "I feel the same way. I'll join you." They prayed from around ten o'clock at night until three o'clock the following morning. They didn't talk with one another, only with God. The following Friday evening, when Billy Ball was scheduled to speak, one of the men who had prayed for hours earlier stood up to speak to the congregation. His spontaneous talk lasted several minutes, then Billy Ball stood up to speak. It was a historic night—a watershed for that church and, as it turned out, a life-changing event for me (though I was at Trevecca some four hundred miles away). It all began with a strong feeling that these men should pray. Nothing more—just pray.

Judgment

The previously mentioned account of Ananias and Sapphira lying to the Holy Spirit brought about a great sense of fear, but this occasion was also a demonstration of the Lord showing up to judge.

A judgment presence of the Lord was in effect when certain people in Corinth were sick and weak and some died. Paul explicitly calls this "judgment" (1 Cor. 11:34, NIV). They had abused the Lord's Supper by disrespecting poor people who could not get to the house church service as early as the more well-to-do Christians. Rather than wait for the poor, the majority went ahead and left the poor people out entirely. God rolled up His sleeves and showed His displeasure. Certain Christians in Corinth were afflicted with illness and even untimely deaths. These people were clearly true Christians. Their being judged showed that they would not be "condemned with the world" (v. 32). And yet a judgment presence of the Lord is not only in operation when sinning people are truly saved.

When I was fifteen, I was in a service in which I believe the Holy Spirit indicated a judgment presence. Eighty-year-old Dr. W. M. Tidwell was the guest evangelist in our Ashland church. During the altar call Dr. Tidwell said something I had not heard before—and haven't heard since: "Someone here is getting their last call." He refused to close the service and turned the service over to the pastor who also would not close the service. People just got up and slowly went to their homes. During the service a teenage girl named Patsy was mocking. My mother remembered it well and wondered at the time if Patsy was the person Dr. Tidwell had in mind. Many recall a great sense of fear settling on the service.

The next day at about five o'clock, as I came home from delivering newspapers, my mother called out, "Did you hear about Patsy?"

"No, what do you mean?"

"She was just killed by a car." A car ran through a stop sign and was hit by an oncoming car and then hit Patsy, who was instantly killed. The effect of those circumstances have lived with me to this day.

Yes, a judgment presence of God had manifested in the service the day before.

Praise

Sometimes we just want to praise the Lord! The Holy Spirit grips us, and the result is spontaneous praise to God. Praising God not only comes easy; it seems natural. We don't have to force it; it flows.

Such a praise presence happened a number of times during Jesus's earthly ministry. When Jesus came into Jerusalem riding on a donkey, a very large crowd of people spread their cloaks and branches on the road. Crowds went ahead of Him, and others followed and shouted, "Hosanna to the Son of David! 'Blessed is He who comes in the name of the Lord!' Hosanna in the highest!" (Matt. 21:9). Even the children were involved in this spontaneous praise (v. 16). This offended the Pharisees. Praise to the Lord Jesus Christ in a noisy and spontaneous manner always offends self-righteous people. The Pharisees said to Jesus, "Teacher, rebuke Your disciples!" (Luke 19:39). He replied, "If these should be silent, the stones would immediately cry out" (v. 40).

Question: Why did God grant a loud praise presence regarding an event that came to nothing within a few days? Answer: The people needed it. God knows the end from the beginning. For our good He grants the kind of manifestation we need at the time. No good thing will He withhold from those whose walk pleases Him (Ps. 84:11).

Loud, noisy praise to God has a long history. People forget this nowadays. When the wall of ancient Jerusalem was dedicated in Ezra's day, they celebrated "with thanks-giving songs and singing, accompanied by cymbals, harps, and lyres" (Neh. 12:27). "From far away the joyful celebration of Jerusalem was heard" (v. 43).

This kind of praise erupted frequently in the early church. "Continuing daily with one mind in the temple, and breaking bread from house to house, they ate their food with gladness and simplicity of heart, praising God and having favor with all the people" (Acts 2:46–47).

And yet praising God is not always easy. This is why the writer speaks of "the sacrifice of praise" (Heb. 13:15), praising God when you don't feel like it. Don't wait until you are "led" to give praise—or until it is spontaneous and easy; do it when you are low, feeling terrible, and have no sense of God's presence. This is a good time to praise God. And I can tell you what often follows: a sense of God's presence. Do it and find it out for yourself!

Insight

To be candid, insight is possibly the kind of manifestation that means most to me. I live for an unfolding of the truth of Scripture I have not seen before. I almost never read a commentary when preparing a sermon. (I check them out if I get stumped or after the sermon is finished, to make sure I haven't gone too far off track!)

Insight may come in one's quiet time. In my case it may come when I am preparing a sermon or singing a hymn. In other words, it may come anytime and at any place— when I'm fishing or even when I'm watching television. I wrote some important chapters of my book *The Thorn in the Flesh* and *The Sensitivity of the Spirit* when I was bonefishing in Key Largo. My understanding of 1 Samuel 16:1—"The LORD said to Samuel, 'How long will you mourn for Saul, since I have rejected him from ruling over Israel? Fill your horn with oil and go. I will send you to Jesse the Bethlehemite, for I have chosen a king for Myself from among his sons'"—came in a split second. In a flash I saw yesterday's man (Saul), today's man (Samuel), and tomorrow's man (David). This insight became the foundation of my book *The Anointing*. It actually came when I could hardly wait to go out fishing! Believe me, insight can come anytime. Another time a needed insight came as I was reaching for my suitcase in the overhead as we were getting ready to exit a plane.

Surprise

God has a way of interrupting our plans. This happened when Peter and John were on their way to the previously mentioned time of prayer—three o'clock in the afternoon. But on their way into the temple they stopped when they came upon a beggar who was disabled, a man who had never walked a day in his life. "Look at us," Peter said to the man (Acts 3:4). He then said, "I have no silver and gold, but I give you what I have. In the name of Jesus Christ of Nazareth, rise up and walk" (v. 6). The man was instantly healed (v. 7). I would call that a most happy interruption.

Dr. Martyn Lloyd-Jones told me how he came to write his book *Spiritual Depression* (one of his greatest but least-known books). "I had planned to start my series of sermons on the Book of Ephesians. As I was getting dressed before church, with only one brace (suspender) over my shoulder, the Lord spoke: 'You are not to begin your series on Ephesians. You are to begin a series on Spiritual Depression.' I was then given the first five topics, and I picked up a piece of paper and wrote them down as fast as I could."

One of my most surprising insights came when I was conducting the Lord's Supper one Sunday evening at Westminster Chapel. I chose the passage that included these words concerning Judas Iscariot, "It would have been good for that man if he had not been born" (Matt. 26:24). In a flash I saw what I had not thought of before: this disproves annihilation regarding eternal punishment. Annihilation means that the person is totally annihilated as though he had never been born. If Judas would be annihilated, Jesus would not have said that; it would mean Judas would not suffer conscious eternal punishment. But he *was* born, and he will be conscious of his betrayal of Jesus throughout eternity.

Expectancy

Sometimes God grants an expectancy presence—a strong sense of hope that something very good is at hand. The New Testament talks about hope as a sense of expectancy that lets you know you will not be disappointed. "Hope does not disappoint," said Paul, because the immediate and direct witness of the Holy Spirit has been given to us (Rom. 5:5).

Many events in the Book of Acts were preceded by a

sense of expectancy. An extraordinary example was when "people brought the sick into the streets and laid them on beds and mats so that at least Peter's shadow might fall on some of them as he passed by" (Acts 5:15, NIV). That is an extraordinary sense of expectancy. And what followed? Were these people disappointed? "Crowds also came out of the cities surrounding Jerusalem, bringing the sick and those who were afflicted by evil spirits, and *they were all healed*" (v. 16, emphasis added).

When Paul was in Corinth, he met opposition from the Jews. He was wondering whether to stay. God said to him: stay. The Lord spoke to him in a vision: "Do not be afraid, but speak and do not be silent. For I am with you, and no one shall attack you and hurt you, for I have many people in this city" (Acts 18:9–10). The phrase "I have many people in this city" refers to God's elect not yet saved but who would be saved. "So for a year and six months he [Paul] sat among them, teaching the word of God" (v. 11). The only way people will be saved is by hearing the word. Faith comes by hearing, and hearing by the word of God (Rom. 10:17).

Gideon was a weak man. He was always in need of encouragement. (See Judges 6:36–40.) God knows our frame; He remembers that we are dust (Ps. 103:14). God knew how to encourage Gideon and give him a spirit of expectancy. Gideon happened to overhear a man telling his dream to someone, which pointed to certain victory for Gideon. This set him ablaze with expectancy. "When Gideon heard the telling of the dream and its interpretation, he worshipped" (Judg. 7:15). He returned to the camp of Israel and charged his men to take the next step in defeating the Midianites. The result was a smashing victory (vv. 15–25).

God knows we all need a sense of expectancy from time to time, and He knows when to provide it. He grants an expectancy presence never too late, never too early, but always just on time.

Direct Guidance

Refer to chapter 4, in which I speak of the "holy nudge" and introduce the acrostic PEACE, for a safe backdrop regarding any sense of guidance. Philip received such guidance; the angel of the Lord said to him, "Rise up and go toward the south on the way that goes down from Jerusalem to Gaza" (Acts 8:26). Then, on his way there, he saw an Ethiopian official in a chariot reading the Book of Isaiah. At that point the Holy Spirit said to Philip, "Go to this chariot and stay with it" (v. 29). Philip's obedience led to the unexpected conversion of the Ethiopian (vv. 26–38).

You will recall how Herod intended to kill Peter as well as James. He put Peter in prison. He was guarded by four squads of four soldiers each. The night before Herod was to bring him to trial—with Peter sleeping between two soldiers, bound with two chains—"an angel of the Lord approached him, and a light shone in the prison. He struck Peter on the side and woke him up, saying, 'Rise up, quickly.' And the chains fell off his hands" (Acts 12:7). Peter was miraculously delivered, passing guards and going through a gate that opened by itself (vv. 8–10).

Nothing is too hard for the Lord. With God all things are possible. God, by His presence, can make anything happen. He has a way of showing up when we least expect Him but need Him most.

Confusion

Could God send confusion? Yes, to His enemies. God is not the author of confusion—or disorder—in the church (1 Cor. 14:33). But one of the ways in which He confronted the enemies of Israel was to send a spirit of confusion to them. This is exactly what He did when the children of Israel crossed the Red Sea. God said, "I will harden the hearts of the Egyptians, so that they shall follow them [the children of Israel], and I will be honored through Pharaoh, through all his army" (Exod. 14:17). So the Egyptians pursued Israel into the sea, and "in the morning watch the Lord looked down on the army of the Egyptians through the pillar of fire and of the cloud and threw the camp of the Egyptians into confusion" (v. 24). The Egyptians were swept into the sea. "Not one of them survived" (v. 28, NIV).

The Lord also caused confusion for the enemies of Gideon and his army. The Israelites shouted, "'A sword for the Lord and for Gideon!' Every man stood in his place all around the camp, but the men in the camp ran, shouted, and fled" (Judg. 7:20–21). Indeed, "the Lord turned every man's sword against his fellow man throughout the camp" (v. 22).

God confused Jonathan's enemies as well. The way Jonathan and his armor bearer revealed themselves to the Philistines took the latter by surprise. Suddenly they killed twenty men in an area of about half an acre (1 Sam.

14:14). "Then panic struck the whole [Philistine] army—those in the camp and field, and those in the outposts and raiding parties—and the ground shook. It was a panic sent by God" (v. 15, NIV).

When King David, having been forced to go into exile, heard that his counselor Ahithophel—known for his unusual wisdom—had sided with Absalom, David prayed, "O LORD, make the advice of Ahithophel folly" (2 Sam. 15:31). God answered David's prayer. "The LORD had decided to undermine the prudent advice of Ahithophel" (2 Sam. 17:14).

I cannot say I have been aware of the Lord causing confusion among those who would hinder His plans for my life. Perhaps He has. Maybe I will discover in heaven how often God did this. In any case, this is something God certainly can do and has done many times for His people.

CHAPTER 9

The Weird and the Wonderful

For My thoughts are not your thoughts, nor
are your ways My ways, says the LORD. For
as the heavens are higher than the earth, so
are My ways higher than your ways, and
My thoughts than your thoughts.
—ISAIAH 55:8–9

But God has chosen the foolish things of the
world to confound the wise. God has chosen
the weak things of the world to confound the
things which are mighty. And God has chosen
the base things of the world and things which
are despised. Yes, and He chose things which
did not exist to bring to nothing things that do,
so that no flesh should boast in His presence.
—1 CORINTHIANS 1:27–29

I HAD JUST BEEN introduced by John Arnott, pastor of Catch the Fire. I took my text for my sermon from Hebrews 4:16: "Let us therefore come boldly unto the throne of grace, that we may obtain mercy, and find grace to help in time of need" (KJV). I have a thirty-year-old sermon based on that passage that I have preached probably a hundred times. I knew it backward and forward; I could preach it anywhere, anytime, at the drop of a hat, without using any notes. But the strangest and weirdest thing happened from the moment I began the sermon. I could not utter a complete intelligible sentence. A heaviness came on me that made it impossible for me to string ten words together. Never in my life—before or since—have I had anything like this happen to me.

I began, "The epistle to the Hebrews..." I could not finish the sentence. "These Hebrew Christians were..." I could not finish. "The writer is addressing..." I tried again and again and again. It was arguably the most embarrassing moment of my life. If someone had offered me ten million dollars' worth of gold bars tax-free to preach that sermon, I still could not have done it. It was physically impossible. Two thousand people in the congregation were laughing their heads off as I tried to preach. My wife, Louise, on the second row was laughing. I was annoyed. I looked at her and said, "Pray for me." My friend Lyndon Bowring was seated next to her. While I pleaded for him to pray, they could not control the laughter. Sweat was pouring down my face. I was not blessed.

Carol Arnott came to the platform and began to pray for me. Someone stood behind me, expecting to catch me when I fell. I stood there erect as the Empire State Building. I was completely unable to utter an intelligible sentence when it came to preaching the sermon. I tried with all the strength and ability I could muster. All I could think of was that this was being recorded and videoed and would get back to Westminster Chapel and my critics. Known for being a Bible expositor, I could hear them saying, "When RT goes to Toronto, he cannot preach, so what does that tell you?" It would be a sign to some that the so-called "Toronto Blessing" was not of God (to put it mildly).

Some fifteen minutes later as I was pleading with the Lord to help me, "Hebrews 13:13" came into my head. I turned in my Bible to see what it was: "Let us go forth therefore unto him without the camp, bearing his reproach" (kjv). I then announced, "Let's try another text," as the crowd laughed all the more. But when I read it, my tongue was loosened. The crowd came to complete silence. I began to preach, and I soared. I am not sure for how long—perhaps twenty minutes or more. I gave an invitation, and more than two hundred people came forward for prayer. I still have people come up to me in various parts of the world who were blessed by what happened that night, some of them saying they were among those who went forward.

What on earth happened? I have asked this question many times. The answer, I think, at least partly, is that God made a change in my text because that was the first day the Toronto church officially and legally went by their new name. They had been disenfranchised by their denomination—the Vineyard fellowship. Until that day they had been the Toronto Airport Vineyard Church. They were ruthlessly and unceremoniously booted out and had to go on *without the camp*. My sermon therefore was a wonderful encouragement to the congregation. It was God giving them a timely endorsement. I would even say—yes—it was a seal of God on the Toronto Blessing. I could not have made that happen in a thousand years. I had no idea what was going on. Whereas the normal phenomenon of this work of the Spirit in Toronto was people helplessly falling to the floor and laughing, the opposite happened with me: I did not fall, and I certainly did not laugh. But there was a heaviness—that is the best word I can come up with—on me that would not let me preach my sermon on Hebrews 4:16. God wanted them to hear a sermon on going on "without the camp" from Hebrews 13:13. For what it's worth, John Wimber, the founder of Vineyard, on his deathbed told John Paul Jackson that the greatest mistake of his life was to disenfranchise the Toronto church.

The "Yuck" Factor

I still get e-mails and letters from people who ask me, "Is it true you have endorsed the Toronto Blessing?" For those who may want to know why I changed my mind, I told the story in my book *Holy Fire* of how I publicly opposed the Toronto blessing and then climbed down publicly after my mind was changed.

The purpose of this chapter is not to defend the Toronto Blessing but to show that God offends the mind to reveal the heart. I have a hypothesis—that God loves to come up with things that will offend the sophisticated. That might include me. When I first heard of people falling to the floor and laughing uproariously at Holy Trinity Brompton, London, I found that offensive, if not disgusting. I also felt somewhat betrayed. Holy Trinity Brompton (HTB) is not only an Anglican church (surely the Church of England is apostate, I have said), but—if that weren't enough—HTB is where some of the staff are privileged Etonians with their distinct, upper-class English accents. I felt that a church such as that is surely the last place God would choose to manifest His true presence. And if God were going to visit the United Kingdom generally and London particularly, He would choose Westminster Chapel. After all, we had borne the "heat of the day" over the years. I put my reputation on the line again and again. I nearly got thrown out of my church for the changes we made, starting with having Arthur Blessitt. I personally was out on the streets of Victoria leading our Pilot Lights, handing out tracts to passersby, singing choruses in our services—which to some was the most offensive thing of all—and giving a public invitation to the lost after preaching the gospel. The thought that God would pass us by and turn to a church like HTB was out of the question.

But I was wrong. God chose to manifest His glory in Westminster Chapel by passing us by and unveiling His presence at the church (surely, I would have said) least likely to inherit His blessing. God's promise to Moses, "I will have mercy on whom I will have mercy" (Exod. 33:19, NIV) and quoted by Paul (Rom. 9:15) is a no-joke matter. The wind of the Holy Spirit blows where it chooses (John 3:8).

So my hypothesis is this—I call it the "yuck" factor: I reckon that God looks high and low over the earth to come up with what will make sophisticated people say "yuck." He does this to see if they will be willing to be humbled by what the world regards as offensive. In Britain particularly, *yuck* is a word to express disgust or repugnance. If people say "yuck" when they see something that appears to make no sense or looks silly, outrageous, or disgusting, God says, "That will do nicely." He continues to choose the foolish things of the world to shame the wise (1 Cor. 1:27). His "ways" are higher than our ways (Isa. 55:9). What God often likes to do makes absolutely no sense at the time—whether His requiring Abraham to sacrifice Isaac (Gen. 22), His commanding King Saul to kill all the Amalekites (1 Sam. 15:3), or Jesus's choosing tax collectors to be His disciples (Matt. 9:9–12). We may or may not like this, but part of God's "ways" is to do things that make no sense at all—at first.

The Purpose of the "Yuck" Factor

God uses the "yuck" factor to promote His glory. He uses it often for lukewarm Christians. Jesus said of the church of Laodicea that they were neither hot nor cold but lukewarm. He wishes Christians would be one or the other. Lukewarm Christians are the hardest to reach and hardest to teach. One way to reach them is to offend the mind to reveal the heart. Jesus promises that He will spit them out of His mouth (Rev. 3:16). Lukewarm Christians make Him sick. One of the characteristics of lukewarm Christians is that they are smug, and God hates smugness. They are self-satisfied, and they have excessive pride in their own achievements. They are pleased with themselves and take themselves very seriously. They would pass a lie detector test in believing they are absolutely in good shape spiritually before God. They see themselves as having need of nothing. The opposite is true, says Jesus. They are "wretched, miserable, poor, blind, and naked" (v. 17).

God sometimes uses people or manifestations that make

us quickly say, "That cannot be God." The "experts" would say the Welsh Revival could not be of God because there was virtually no preaching and all spontaneous singing. John Wesley was offended with George Whitefield leaving the pulpit and going to the fields to preach to ordinary people. And when the hearers of Whitefield jerked or barked like dogs as he preached, that—to Wesley—was undeniable proof that such manifestations were not of God. But eventually Wesley followed Whitefield to the fields and saw the same manifestations.

"They have not known My ways," God said of ancient Israel (Heb. 3:10). Those of us who see God's "ways" only in terms of His sovereignty, transcendence, majesty, and glory are often the first to be critical of manifestations that seems to be utterly disgraceful—laughing, shouting, jumping, running, and rolling on the floor. There is a reason some were called "holy rollers"; people literally *rolled* on the floor, carpet, or ground. Yes, it is indeed one of God's ways to bring people to reverence, submission, and fear. And, amusingly enough, I have had people say "yuck" over my preaching of the sovereignty of God! But it is also one of God's ways to challenge our dignity through strange manifestations. I can tell you, God has humbled me.

Finding Your Friends

David was very excited when he finally succeeded in bringing the ark of the covenant to Jerusalem. Some might say he truly went over the top. Wearing a linen ephod, he "danced before the LORD with all of his might...."

So David and the whole house of Israel escorted the ark of the LORD with shouting and the sound of the horn" (2 Sam. 6:14). But his own wife Michal, the daughter of King Saul, was offended. "When she saw King David leaping and dancing before the LORD, she despised him in her heart" (v. 16, NIV). So when David arrived at home, he got a tongue-lashing of no mean proportion. "How the king of Israel has dignified himself today, exposing himself this day in the sight of his servant's slave girls like one of the rabble might shamelessly expose himself" (v. 20). David's reply is so amazing. Instead of being embarrassed and backing down, he said to her:

> It was before the LORD, who chose me over your father and over everyone in his household, to appoint me ruler over the people of the LORD, over Israel. I was celebrating before the LORD. I will humble myself even more than this and be abased in my own eyes. But by the maidservants, of whom you have spoken, I will be held in honor.
>
> —2 SAMUEL 6:21–22

The New International Version translates a portion of this as "I will become even more undignified than this"! Extraordinary. I love it. This was one of David's finest hours. He was unashamed before these servant girls. He did not apologize for getting carried away. I called my sermon "Finding Your Friends" when I preached on this passage (now in my book *A Man After God's Own Heart*). One of Matt Redman's best songs, "Undignified," is based on this scripture of being even more undignified.

Who are your friends? Are they the ones who question

your wisdom because you are doing all within your heart to glorify God? Or could it be that your true friends are not those who will get you a prestigious invitation, but those who are sold out to the praise and honor of God? Such people are your friends.

One of the stigmas in embracing the weird manifestations of God's presence is not merely refusing to apologize for these manifestations; it is not rejecting those *people* whose lack of dignity and sophistication could well cause embarrassment. Tell me about it! "The flakes you have with you always," a friend of mine once observed. My own greatest challenge was in the days we had Arthur Blessitt or John Arnott in our pulpit. But in the same vein of Paul's caution to Timothy, not to be "ashamed...of me, His prisoner" (2 Tim. 1:8), we must take the less desirable with the more acceptable manifestations.

John Wesley rebuked George Whitefield for tolerating the wildness of some of his followers. "You know a lot of this is of the flesh," said Wesley to him—referring to things like the barking and jerking.

"Agreed," said Whitefield.

Wesley then lectured him, "Then stamp out what is false."

Whitefield replied: "If you stamp out what is of the flesh, you will also kill what is real. You have to let them alone." It is much the same as letting the wheat and tares (or weeds) grow together (Matt. 13:29–30).

No Apologies From Jesus

I find it interesting that Jesus did not apologize for saying that people must eat His flesh and drink His blood (John 6:53). His followers said, "This is a hard teaching. Who can accept it?" (John 6:60, NIV). This was so revolting that many of His followers "went back and walked no more with Him" (v. 66). When Jesus saw the crowds deserting Him, He did not panic. He did not shout to the crowd, "Wait. Please don't leave. Let Me explain. I was referring to what will be called Holy Communion." No. He let them think what they wanted to think.

The same is true of His saying, "Destroy this temple, and in three days I will raise it up" (John 2:19). He let His critics assume He was talking about the building on the Temple Mount. He did not add, "Oh, by the way, I am talking about My resurrection from the dead." But that is what He meant! (See John 2:21–22.)

When at Westminster Chapel, if we had an Arthur Blessitt or a Randy Clark there, the strangest people I ever saw in my life would come out of the woodwork from all over London. They would take the front seats and wave their arms in the air as if to show us the proper way to worship. I would die a thousand deaths every time they would show up, but I never said a word to them, difficult though it was to remain silent. I knew they wanted to draw attention to themselves and that they felt they were a cut above the rest of us when it came to worshipping God.

Part of the stigma of many moves of the Holy Spirit is that there will be embarrassing excesses. A stigma is offensive, and it comes down to one word: *embarrass-ment*. Jesus in effect said to the Twelve, "Does this offend [embarrass] you?" (John 6:61). Jesus then asked them, noting that the crowd of five thousand had deserted Him, whether they too would leave Him. After all, when you are a part of something big—like Jesus having five thousand supporters—the stigma of following Jesus is lessened. But when five thousand dwindles down to twelve, the test becomes very severe. Peter, however, passed the test that time. He replied: "Lord, to whom shall we go? You have the words of eternal life" (v. 68).

How to Endure Criticism

I have managed to endure the criticisms of those sincere—and sometimes godly—people who doubt my wisdom when it comes to endorsing strange manifestations. I ask myself one question: What would I do if I knew that I would stand before Jesus at the judgment seat in the next twenty-four hours? That makes the challenge dissolve to nothing. When I know in my heart I am not afraid to face Him, I know I am on safe ground in endorsing the weird manifestations that are going to come with every authentic move of the Spirit. But I would certainly hate to stand before Him if I had capitulated to the fear of people. What is more, the fear of man is a snare (Prov. 29:25). Not all who oppose weird manifestations are afraid of people, but some of them are. I refuse to be among them.

We live in a generation in which people want to destig-matize the gospel. They would rob it of its glory—denying that the God-man satisfied God's justice by His most precious blood. There are also those who would destigmatize the Holy Spirit—only affirming what keeps them in their comfort zone.

The previously mentioned story about the unusual service in my old church in Ashland, Kentucky, helped to pave the way for the kind of decisions I would have to make many years later. It is another example of a judgment presence of God. That service changed my life, although I was not present at it. I now reveal more of the story. Having prayed for several hours the previous Thursday night and Friday morning, these men interrupted the service that followed that Friday evening.

While the congregation were singing the hymn "The Unclouded Day," one man named Ed, a layman who owned his own business, asked the song leader to stop singing and organist to stop playing. They did. The man was not highly educated, but with boldness that took everyone by surprise, he began speaking spontaneously to a stilled congregation of some four hundred people, walking back and forth in the front and up and down the center aisle. Many present were horrified, including my father; they said he merely raved and ranted like a madman for several minutes. Others saw it as the presence of the Holy Spirit and felt that God was dealing with them. Ed said basically two things: that someone in the church was holding up the revival that God wanted the church to have, and that God had written "Ichabod," which means "the glory has departed," over the church. As Ed spoke, a haze—a visible cloud—settled on the people, troubling him, for he had no idea what the haze was, nor did he have a clue what Ichabod meant.

The associate pastor was scheduled to speak. When Ed sat down, the associate pastor stood and said from the pulpit, "This is the greatest demonstration of the Holy Ghost I have ever seen." He read the account of Ananias in Acts 5:1–6, who had been struck dead for lying to the Holy Spirit. He then sat down. The senior pastor of the church walked to the pulpit and invited people to come to the altar to pray. Several did. Some said they were converted that night, and some worried that they could be the very ones holding up the revival. Who it actually was, however, surfaced two days later.

On the following Sunday, the associate pastor was asked to resign his position. He was accused of orchestrating the service in which Ed had the leading role. This was not true, although he clearly endorsed what Ed did and said. My father wrote me a letter the following Monday in which he warned me not to have anything to do with the associate pastor, who had been a mentor to me. "Do not write him, do not phone him, have nothing to do with him," my dad said. I was shaken rigid. I had not heard about the unusual service. However, as soon as I read my father's letter, "Philippians 1:12" came into my head. I quickly turned to it. It read: "I would ye should understand, brethren, that the things which happened to me have fallen out rather unto the furtherance of the gospel" (KJV). I knew instantly from that verse that I would have to stand by my mentor. It was the first breach I had with my dad. It was also no small ingredient in my grandmother's decision to take my car back.

When I later heard about the haze, I knew it was the visible presence of God. I took it as a seal on Philippians

1:12 and that God was undoubtedly the instigator of this strange service. I have never looked back, nor have I doubted the decision I took to stand with those two men. Because people are still living who are related to some of the people involved in this story—especially those related to the person who allegedly had stopped the revival, I cannot say more—except this: my old church was never the same again. The glory had departed. What was once regarded as one of the most influential churches in the entire denomination of the Church of the Nazarene gradually went down, down, down from that day on.

It was this service—probably more than my theological change—that caused most of my family to turn against me. That service in April 1956 was *way* outside their comfort zone. Those were difficult days. As I said earlier, I had one relative—my grandpa McCurley—who stood by me. "I'm for him, right or wrong," he said.

The Quintessence of God's Rest

> LORD, my heart is not haughty, my eyes are not raised too high. I have not striven for enormities, for things too wonderful for me. I composed and quieted my desire, like a child given suck by his mother; like a child who sucks is my desire within me.
>
> —PSALM 131:1–2

Psalm 131 is a psalm of ascent. It belongs to a group of psalms the people of Israel sang three times a year as they made their pilgrimages to Jerusalem. Because Jerusalem is something like 2,500 feet above sea level, all roads to Jerusalem went "up"; hence they are called psalms of ascent. Psalm 131 is unique and difficult to grasp, but I have come to see at least two possible interpretations of it.

First, it describes David toward the end of his life. He had ceased to be the ambitious type A personality that characterized him for most of his life. When you read Psalm 131 with this perspective, it makes sense. David was not concerned with the things that used to motivate him. Such a psalm therefore might apply to those highly motivated people who wanted to make an impact on their generation, who were great achievers—the movers and shakers of the world. When people come toward the end of their lives, they see things very differently. "I have composed and quieted my desire" (v. 2). This is the position I took in my book *Higher Ground*, a book on the psalms of ascent.

Second, probably the main meaning of Psalm 131 is that it perfectly describes a person who has entered into God's rest. The one who enters God's rest will "cease from his own works" (Heb. 4:10). Such individuals cease to strive. Ambition is almost entirely diminished. Trying to reach goals is not so important. They no longer take themselves so seriously; they don't consider their lives so dear (Acts 20:24; Rev. 12:11). The presence of God is so fulfilling in itself that those who enter God's rest have no need to prove themselves. Brother Lawrence, to whom I refer below, would speak of getting as much joy from picking up a piece of straw from the ground as speaking to thousands. This is the wonderful thing about entering God's rest: a sense of His presence is so satisfying that the need to be seen or heard or taken seriously is put aside.

How long this sense of the presence of God lasts is another matter. Some enjoy it for months, some for years, but few enjoy it indefinitely. And yet Brother Lawrence seemed to enjoy it throughout his lifetime.

Brother Lawrence (c. 1614–1691)

Brother Lawrence, born as Nicolas Herman in what is now France, was an uneducated Roman Catholic lay monk. He served in the Thirty Years' War before applying to belong to the Discalced Carmelite Priory in Paris. He stayed there for most of his life, and for many years he worked in the kitchen, but he was a repairer of sandals later on in his life. He is well known for experiencing profound peace, so much so that many visitors and church leaders looked to him for wisdom and guidance.[1]

Some of Brother Lawrence's letters and reports of conversations were published by the vicar general of the archbishop of Paris under the title *The Practice of the Presence of God*, becoming popular with both Protestants and Catholics. The book was commended by John Wesley and A. W. Tozer. I came across a ragged copy of it in 1955. I often carried it with me and have turned to it many times. There were occasions when it spoke definitely to me. I identified with it mainly because Brother Lawrence's descriptions of peace and sense of God's presence sounded like what I had initially experienced in 1955. The phrase "practice of the presence of God" is his.

"Were I a preacher, I would above all other things preach the practice of the presence of God. Were I a director, I should advise all the world to do it, so necessary do I think it, and so easy too."[2] Easy? Yes, but perhaps not all who try to do this experience the same sense of God's presence as Brother Lawrence evidently did. The main word seems to be *peace*. This peace was not merely the absence of anxiety but the presence of a supernatural sense of God. God is called the "God of peace" (1 Thess. 5:23), this being a description of Him; the phrase "peace of God" (Phil. 4:7) is a description of His presence. Paul says this peace "surpasses all understanding" and also *guards* our hearts and minds in Christ Jesus (v. 7).

When reading *The Practice of the Presence of God*, one must keep in mind the fact that Brother Lawrence was uneducated. He would never have been accepted as a cleric but only as a layperson in his monastery. His statements not only do not always match the purest theology, but his ability to describe what he senses does not always make sense! But if one is willing to throw aside biases, we can see that this French monk was in touch with the God of the Bible in a wonderful way. What strikes me is his testimony that the set times of prayer and worship did not bring him closer to God. This was because he already felt the presence of God all the time. For one thing, he claimed that his conversion at the age of eighteen immediately "set him loose from the world, and kindled in him such a love for God, that he could not tell whether it had increased during the more than forty years he had lived since." Brother Lawrence established such a connection through time spent praying: "We should establish ourselves in a sense of God's Presence by continually conversing with him. It was a shameful thing to quit His conversation to think of trifles and fooleries." He said we ought to "seek our satisfaction only in the fulfilling of His will. Whether God lead us by suffering or by consolation, all would be equal to a soul truly resigned." We need to be faithful "in those disruptions in the ebb and flow of prayer when God tries our love to Him. This was the time for a complete act of resignation."[3] Brother Lawrence reveals his deep faith in the sovereignty of God, as reported in one of his conversations with a Catholic cardinal:

> He said that as far as the miseries and sins he heard of daily in the world, he was so far from wondering at them, that, on the contrary, he was surprised there were not more considering the malice sinners were capable of. For his part, he prayed for them. But knowing that God could remedy the mischief they did when He pleased, he gave himself no further trouble.[4]

If Brother Lawrence should fail in his duty, he only confessed his fault, saying to God, "I shall never do otherwise if You leave me to myself; it is You must hinder my falling, and mend what is amiss." After that "he gave himself no further uneasiness about it." We should, with no anxiety, "expect the pardon of our sins from the blood of Jesus Christ only endeavoring to love Him with all our hearts. And he noted that God seemed to have granted the greatest favors to the greatest sinners as more signal monuments of His mercy." The "time of business," he said, "does not with me differ from the time of prayer. In the noise and clatter of my kitchen, while several persons are at the same time calling for different things, I possess

God in as great tranquility is if I were upon my knees at the Blessed Supper."[5]

I close this chapter with a reminder that one of God's ways is to do things that are initially misunderstood and make no sense at first. The greatest example of this? Good Friday. Who would have thought at that time and on that day that God was in Christ reconciling the world to Himself (2 Cor. 5:19)? But God Himself was at work. The way God chose to save us was the best kept secret in human history—until the early church made it known.

This should give each of us pause. We must lower our voices and wait and see whether God is actually the instigator of the very things that offend us. Until we know for sure that God is *not* in certain manifestations and movements, let us be wary of fighting against them lest we fight against God!

CHAPTER 10

The Presence of God in Heaven

I desire to depart and be with
Christ, which is better by far.
—PHILIPPIANS 1:23, NIV

I heard a loud voice from heaven, saying, "Look!
The tabernacle of God is with men, and He will
dwell with them. They shall be His people, and
God Himself will be with them and be their
God. 'God shall wipe away all tears from their
eyes. There shall be no more death.' Neither
shall there be any more sorrow nor crying nor
pain, for the former things have passed away."
—REVELATION 21:3–4

THAT WHICH WILL make heaven *heaven* is the presence
of God. When we get to heaven, we will not need to
pursue His presence; His presence will be manifest from
the moment we are glorified. This glorification takes place
when we see Jesus face-to-face (1 John 3:2). There will be
no tears, no trials, no temptation, no insecurities, and
no hiding of God's face. We will have no need for faith.
Whereas faith is the assurance of things not seen (Heb.

11:1), in heaven we shall see things clearly without having to exercise faith.

In this present world we are urged to "seek the LORD while He may be found," and call "upon Him while He is near" (Isa. 55:6). In this life "let all the faithful pray to [God] while [He] may be found" (Ps. 32:6, NIV). But this effort will not be needed in heaven. His manifest presence will be everywhere. There will be no hiding of His face in heaven. What will make heaven *heaven* is the presence of the Lord.

When I was a boy, a variety of songs were written about heaven. These songs varied from an emphasis on "mansions," based on John 14:2—"In my Father's house are many mansions" (KJV)—to living in a cabin. One could sing "Mansion Over the Hilltop"—as sung by Elvis Presley—and "Lord Build Me a Cabin in the Corner of Glory"—as sung by Hank Williams. The latter song, I suspect, expressed the Uriah Heep spirit of the Appalachians; the false humility suggests "I don't need a mansion; I'll be content with a cabin."

What will make heaven *heaven* is not the luxury of our new dwelling place, living where there are streets of pure gold, but God's presence. Now we see through a glass darkly, but in heaven we will see face-to-face (1 Cor. 13:12). We need faith now, but we won't need it then.

Charles Gabriel wrote a song about what heaven will be like:

Oh that will be glory for me,
Glory for me, glory for me,

When by His grace I shall look on His face,
That will be glory, be glory for me.[1]

It is impossible to imagine what experiencing such glory will be like. Forty years ago I signed a contract with an evangelical publisher to write a book on heaven; Dr. Martyn Lloyd-Jones witnessed my signature! But later I had to get released from the contract because I began writing it and then realized how little I knew about the subject. It is, I think, the only book I never finished.

We will learn a lot more about heaven five minutes after we get there. This much I can say with certainty: "I consider that the sufferings of this present time are not worthy to be compared with the glory which shall be revealed to us" (Rom. 8:18). As another hymn proclaims, "Just one glimpse of Him in glory will the toils of life repay!"[2]

Transition to Heaven

Our transition from earth to heaven will come in one of two ways. First, death. This would be in advance of the eschaton—the final day. According to Paul, we get our *spiritual* bodies when we die. "We know that if our earthly house, this tent, were to be destroyed, we have an eternal building of God in the heavens, a house not made with hands" (2 Cor. 5:1). This is a temporary abode, and yet it will be very like our final glorification. I say this because we come to God, "the Judge of all; and to the spirits of the righteous ones made perfect" (Heb. 12:23). Truly this will be like glorification: there will be no sin. Our spiritual bodies will be without sin because there can be no sin in heaven. Our permanent transformed bodies will come later, to which I shall return. In the meantime we may be sure we will have spiritual bodies in heaven the moment we die. Moses and Elijah appeared with Jesus when He was transformed (Matt. 17:3). This shows they have recognizable identities—bodies—now in heaven. We may take this to indicate that our friends and loved ones who have gone to heaven already have recognizable bodies and have spirits made perfect. We may assume therefore that all of us will have this kind of dwelling the moment we die.

Jesus said to the dying thief on the cross, "Truly, I tell you, today you will be with Me in Paradise" (Luke 23:43). He meant that only a few hours later the thief would be in His presence in "Paradise"—a name given to the place of the sainted dead.

This, however, is a temporary abode, though it would mean an abode of thousands of years for Abraham, Isaac, Jacob, Joseph, and Moses, hundreds of years for Martin Luther, John Calvin, Jonathan Edwards, John Wesley, and George Whitefield, and dozens of years for my parents and Dr. and Mrs. Martyn Lloyd-Jones. But they are all together as you read these lines. They are conscious, pain-free, secure in the arms of Jesus, and enjoying the immediate presence of Jesus. To ponder how well these people get to know each other in heaven—or how much they may know about us here on earth—is to engage in unprofitable speculation. It is fun to think about as long as we don't take our views too seriously.

But this much I believe: the moment we die, we consciously enter the presence of Jesus.

Second, we will enter our final abode at Jesus's second coming. At this time our *physical* bodies will be resurrected.

"We shall all be changed. In a moment, in the twinkling of an eye, at the last trumpet, for the trumpet will sound, the dead will be raised incorruptible, and we shall be changed" (1 Cor. 15:51–52). Jesus said, "Do not marvel at this. For the hour is coming in which all who are in the graves will hear His voice and come out—those who have done good to the resurrection of life, and those who have done evil to the resurrection of the judgment" (John 5:28–29). The Bible is silent on the nature of the resurrected bodies of the lost. We only know that all men and women who ever lived will be raised to stand judgment. It is appointed unto humankind once to die, "after this comes the judgment" (Heb. 9:27). Even "the sea gave up the dead who were in it" (Rev. 20:13). This proves that it does not matter whether one had a traditional burial, was cremated, or died at sea. The Creator God will transform all bodies. In any case, once Jesus comes, "so we shall be forever with the Lord" (1 Thess. 4:17). The phrase "with the Lord" means *with Jesus*. We will be in the presence of our Lord Jesus Christ forever and ever.

What Happens to the Lost

What about the lost? Where do they go? I reply in much the same way as above. First, when they die: if the account of the rich man and Lazarus indicates anything, it demonstrates that when people die, they go immediately—consciously—to bliss or punishment. Lazarus the beggar died and went to "Abraham's presence" (Luke 16:22). This would be the equivalent of Paradise as we saw above in the case of the dying thief on the cross. The reference to Abraham probably means that the patriarchs—Abraham, Isaac, and Jacob—are alive and well, as Jesus demonstrated to the Sadducees (Matt. 22:32). This again shows the spirit of righteous men made perfect, as in Hebrews 12:23, and further demonstrates that when we die and go to be with the Lord, we will join a multitude of the sainted dead (Heb. 12:1).

However, the rich man also died and was buried. The next thing we read is: "In Hades, being in torment, he lifted up his eyes and saw Abraham from a distance and Lazarus in his presence" (Luke 16:23). The rich man begged Abraham, "Send Lazarus to dip the tip of his finger in water and cool my tongue. For I am tormented in this flame" (v. 24). The rich man's predicament indicates conscious punishment for the unsaved immediately after they die.

I am aware of the teaching of "soul sleep"—that people are not conscious when they die, whether saved or lost. This—to me—is but to superimpose a philosophical judgment on the previously mentioned scriptures that encourage us to believe that the saved and lost are equally conscious after they die.

But is the state of the lost a temporary abode as in the case of the saved? Yes. The lost will be raised and given permanent bodies at the Second Coming. This is when they will face the final judgment. At His second coming the Lord Jesus will take vengeance "on those who do not know God and do not obey the gospel of our Lord Jesus Christ. They shall be punished with eternal destruction, isolated from the presence of the Lord and from the glory of His power, when He comes, in that Day, to be glorified in His saints and to be marveled at by all those who believe, because our testimony among you was believed" (2 Thess. 1:8–10).

If what makes heaven *heaven* is the presence of the Lord, then what will make hell *hell* will be to be "isolated from the presence of the Lord" (2 Thess. 1:9). Partly what will make hell *hell* will be having to see what one missed— namely, when Jesus is "glorified in His saints" and "marveled at by all those who believe" (v. 10). As the rich man saw what he missed by seeing Lazarus at Abraham's side, so will all the lost have to gaze on what they missed by rejecting the gospel.

The eternally lost will not only miss out on what the saved get to enjoy, but they will lose all the benefits of God's common grace. This is not ordinary grace but rather God's goodness given commonly to all people—saved or lost. Here on earth both saved and lost enjoy the sun and the rain—gifts of God's grace to all people (Matt. 5:45). The lost will forfeit these blessings. They will be "shut out" from the presence of the Lord.

Experiencing God's Presence in Heaven

At the beginning of this book I told about my friend having a sense of the presence of God that was so wonderful he would be willing to endure "anything" just for that moment. These things said, whatever will it be like when we have that sense of God throughout eternity? It is mind-boggling and dazzling to say the least. It all seems too good to be true. But that is what heaven will be like, only that we will realize how true it is. Jesus said, "If it were not so, I would have told you" (John 14:2).

But it *is* so! Heaven is the end of death, the end of having to pay bills, the end of fighting off illness and disease, the end of saying good-bye to our loved ones, the end of struggle, the end of trial and temptation, the end of being misunderstood, the end of vindication withheld, the end of worry and anxiety, and the end of whatever is painful.

Yes. It does seem too good to be true, doesn't it? But it is true. I would go to the stake for what I have written in this chapter and in this book.

The big question is, do you know for sure that if you were to die today that you would go to heaven? Do you? And if you were to stand before God—and you will—and He were to ask you—and He might—"Why should I let you into my heaven?," what would you say? What comes to your mind? Suppose all this were very, very real—and you had to come up with the right answer—and there is only one answer, what would you say?

I will tell you what I would say: "Jesus died on the cross for my sins." This is literally my only hope—not my good works, not my role as a husband, father, or minister. I have one hope: the death of Jesus on the cross. His blood paid my debt. His sinless life and sacrificial death satisfied God's justice.

If this is not your hope, please pray this prayer:

> *Lord Jesus, I need You. I want You. I am sorry
> for my sins. Wash my sins away by Your blood. I
> welcome Your Holy Spirit into my life. As best
> as I know how, I give You my life. Amen.*

If you prayed that prayer—and meant it in your heart, I will see you in heaven where we can enjoy the presence of the Lord forever and ever.

May the triune God—Father, Son and Holy Spirit—abide with you now and ever more. Amen.

Notes

Chapter 2. When God Hides His Face

1. *Vine's Complete Expository Dictionary of Old and New Testament Words: With Topical Index*, ed. W. E. Vine and Merrill Unger (Nashville: Thomas Nelson, 1996), s.v. "scourge."

2. "Lord of All Being" by Oliver W. Holmes Sr. Public domain.

3. "How Tedious and Tasteless the Hours" by John Newton. Public domain.

4. I have gone into detail on the subject of terminal chastening in two books: *The Judgment Seat of Christ* and *Are You Stone Deaf to the Spirit or Rediscovering God?*, both published by Christian Focus, UK.

Chapter 4. The Holy Nudge

1. "Yogi Berra Quotes," Brainy Quote, accessed February 2, 2017, https://www.brainyquote.com/quotes/quotes/y/yogiberra110034.html.

Chapter 6. Integrity

1. Mark Galli, "Revival at Cane Ridge," *Christianity Today*, accessed February 6, 2017, http://www.christianitytoday.com/history/issues/issue-45/revival-at-cane-ridge.html.

2. R. T. Kendall, "Sheer Integrity," *Ministry Today*, June 30, 2008, accessed February 16, 2017, http://ministry

todaymag.com/evangelical-essentials/17445-sheer
-integrity.

3. Upton Sinclair, *I, Candidate for Governor: And How I
    Got Licked* (Los Angeles: University of California Press,
    1994), 109.

4. Robert Frost, "The Road Not Taken, Commonlit,
    accessed February 15, 2017, https://www.commonlit
    .org/texts/the-road-not-taken.

5. Winston S. Churchill, "The Gift of a Common
    Tongue," The International Churchill Society, Sep-
    tember 6, 1943, accessed February 6, 2017, http://www
    .winstonchurchill.org/resources/speeches/1941-1945-war
    -leader/420-the-price-of-greatness-is-responsibility.

Chapter 9. The Weird and the Wonderful

1. Brother Lawrence, Christian Classics Ethereal Library,
    accessed February 16, 2017, https://www.ccel.org/ccel
    /lawrence.

2. Brother Lawrence, *The Practice of the Presence of God*
    (N.p.: Lightheart, 2002).

3. Ibid.

4. Ibid.

5. Ibid.

Chapter 10. The Presence of God in Heaven

1. "Oh, That Will Be Glory" by Charles H. Gabriel.
    Public domain.

2. "When We All Get to Heaven" by Eliza F. Hewitt.
    Public domain.

Other Books by R. T. Kendall:

The Anointing
Prepare Your Heart for the Midnight Cry
Controlling the Tongue
Pure Joy
In Pursuit of His Glory
In Pursuit of His Wisdom
Pigeon Religion: Holy Spirit, Is That You?
It Ain't Over Till It's Over
The Sensitivity of the Spirit
Imitating Christ
Holy Fire
The Thorn in the Flesh
The Word and the Spirit
Grace
40 Days With the Holy Spirit
How to Forgive Ourselves—Totally
When God Shows Up
The Unfailing Love of Jesus
God Gives Second Chances
Totally Forgiving God
Did You Think to Pray?
Jealousy—The Sin No One Talks About
The Power of Humility
Total Forgiveness
By Love Transformed
Just Say Thanks
Worshipping God
Total Forgiveness Experience
A Man After God's Own Heart
Finding Your Heart's Desire
Word Spirit Power
Unashamed to Bear His Name

The Christian and the Pharisee
God Meant It for Good
The Parables of Jesus

CONNECT WITH US!

CHARISMA HOUSE

(Spiritual Growth)

Facebook.com/CharismaHouse

@CharismaHouse

Instagram.com/CharismaHouse

SILOAM

(Health)

Pinterest.com/CharismaHouse

MEV MODERN ENGLISH VERSION

(Bible)

www.mevbible.com